Tom Fox Was My Friend.
Yours, Too.

Passages for Reflection and Study

Compiled and Edited by
Chuck Fager

Kimo Press

In Association with
The Religious Education Committee of
Baltimore Yearly Meeting of
The Religious Society of Friends

NOTE: Tom's complete blog and some additional emails, can be
found online at: http://waitinginthelight.blogspot.com/

ISBN 0-945177-50-X

First published 2006
Reissued 2016

Kimo Press
P.O. Box 3811
Durham NC 27702
www.afriendlyletter.com

George Fox

> "Be patterns, be examples in every country, place, or nation that you visit, so that your bearing and life might communicate with all people. Then you'll walk cheerfully across the earth answering that of God in everyone. So that you will be seen as a blessing in their eyes and you will receive a blessing from that of God within them."

From the Epistle to the Hebrews

> 13:3: Remember those who are in prison, as though you were in prison with them; those who are being tortured, as though you yourselves were being tortured.

From the Qur'an

> 11:20: And all that We relate to you of the news of the Messengers is in order that We may make strong and firm your heart thereby.

> 12:111: Indeed in their stories there is a lesson for men and women of understanding.

From the Tao Te Ching

> Nothing in the world is as soft and yielding as water, yet nothing can better overcome the hard and strong, for they can neither control nor do away with it. The soft overcomes the hard, the yielding overcomes the strong. Everyone knows this, but who can practice it?

Contents

How to Use This Book

In his tribute to Tom, Norman Kember recalled that during their long tedious days of captivity, Tom often led impromptu Bible study sessions, on scripture passages recited as accurately as they could remember them. Their discussions of these passages followed a pattern, Kember said, "of first impressions, relevance to our life experience, difficulties in understanding and how the message would change our life."

In his blog and emails, Tom Fox was certainly not writing scripture. But let me suggest following a similar pattern in using this little book. Each section here includes a passage by or about Tom, paired with a response or commentary. In a group, the sections could be read aloud, then discussed in turn as to the hearers' first impressions, the possible relevance to our lives, our difficulties in understanding or relating to what was written, and how – or whether– what's there might change our lives. The pattern would be similar for private reading and reflection.

Are such exercises worthwhile? Consider: Tom Fox ended up dead on a Baghdad trash heap in large measure because he acted on a belief that, as Jesus said in the Gospel of John: "Very truly, I tell you, unless a grain of wheat falls into the earth and dies, it remains just a single grain; but if it dies, it bears much fruit." (12:24)

Is such a conviction just a doomed do-gooder's fantasy? The answers to this question will come from you, the person holding and sharing these pages.

Introduction

I

John Stephens called me with the news: Tom Fox and three other members of the Christian peacemaker Teams' group in Baghdad had been kidnaped. In the summer of 2005 John was an intern at Quaker House in Fayetteville, North Carolina, where I am Director. When he was applying for an internship, I asked him for a letter of reference; the reference came by email from Tom Fox, in Baghdad.

John describes in his essay how he knew Tom. I met Tom in the early 1990s at Langley Hill Friends meeting in McLean, Virginia, where we were both members. I didn't know him especially well, but his children were the same ages as my younger two, and the four of them grew up in that meeting, conspiring to torment a generation of First Day School teachers, on many a weekend morning. Tom was also very kind to me at some moments of personal need.

Tom's path to Iraq and an ignominious death was straightforward. We talked about it in August, 2005 when I saw him for the final time.

It was at the annual sessions of Baltimore Yearly Meeting, our regional Quaker conference, in Harrisonburg Virginia.

Spiritually, Baltimore Yearly Meeting had long been home to both of us. The body operates three summer camps, and Tom had been active with them, serving as cook at one. He had also been a "Friendly Adult Presence" (or FAP) with the yearly meeting's youth group, even filling in as interim youth staffperson for a period. At the yearly meeting sessions, he frequently worked with the children's program. Indeed, if it had not been for his leading toward CPT and Iraq, any biography of Tom would have been much more about youth work than peace witness as such.

When we met in Harrisonburg in 2005, Tom was between tours in Iraq, and we shared a meal and did some catching up.

We talked first about kids, as older dads will do. His

Andrew and Kassie, my Guli and Asa, are in their twenties now, scattered across the continent, but still in touch. A few years back, our sons started a Quaker Hip Hop group called the Friendly Gangstaz Committee. The band caused quite a stir in our small, staid Quaker world, with its startling, shouted renditions of well-worn hymns like "Simple Gifts." Tom and I chuckled ruefully about that.

We also talked about work. From that same faith community, Tom and I had traveled somewhat parallel paths, trying to be true to the meaning of texts like, "Blessed are the peacemakers,"(Matthew 5:9) and "seek peace and pursue it."(Proverbs 34:14)

How do you "pursue peace" in a violent world? My own seeking had led, after a series of conventional jobs, to Fayetteville and Quaker House, a long-standing peace project hard by Fort Bragg, one of the largest U.S. military bases.

Tom had grown up in Chattanooga, Tennessee, then did twenty years in the Marine band in Washington DC, playing bass clarinet – about as unmilitary a soldier as one could feature. He began attending Friends meetings during this time. After the Marine band, he became a baker and manager at a growing health food supermarket. He was good at this, and his bosses wanted him to move up in management.

But Tom heard a "different drummer," especially after September 11, 2001. With a war on, he felt called to "pursue peace" in a concrete way. After much prayer and reflection, he joined the Christian Peacemaker Teams (CPT).

CPT sets out to bring the "weapons of the spirit" into the front lines of conflict, places where death and life are but a hair's breadth apart. Tom's first assignment took him to Iraq. For a respite, he visited the Occupied Territories of Palestine.

This was dangerous work, in a region where conflicts seem hopelessly intractable. Tom stuck with it. Then, as the Iraq occupation shifted from the foolish illusion of "mission accomplished" to the grinding facts of guerilla and civil war, he headed back there.

After Tom was kidnaped, along with Canadians James Loney and Harmeet Sooden, and British pacifist Norman Kember, conservative radio host Rush Limbaugh sneered that "part of me likes this," because, "I like any time a bunch of leftist feel-good hand-wringers are shown reality."

What's striking in this comment is not only the mean-spiritedness, but also the ignorance. Tom certainly knew the reality of Baghdad's dangers, firsthand. He talked frankly about them over that last August supper. Tom was calm but clear about it: kidnaping, torture, murder were daily fare on all sides there. How could he be so offhand about it?

I don't know, except to say: that was Tom.

Illusions? Not in CPT. It was a CPT team, after all, that brought the first reports about the abuses at Abu Ghraib prison to reporter Seymour Hersh. They had also seen other humanitarian workers kidnaped and some killed.

But there's more to it than simply experience. The Christian Peacemaker Teams take their identity seriously. Their namesake, after all, was another unarmed troublemaker in an occupied country, who was tortured and then suffered an ignominious public execution. One other phrase that comes to mind is Matthew 10:24: "The disciple is not above his master, nor the servant above his lord."

II

But such quotations roll too easily off the tongue. When John Stephens called about the kidnaping, I wanted Tom and his colleagues released, safely, and NOW. But what, John and I asked each other, could we do to help free them?

We kept coming back to this question in the next few days – and we were not the only ones – as a deadline for the captives' execution approached. Experts in crisis situations advised informally that the best approach was to raise the prisoners' public profile, and seek as much public outcry for their safety as possible. That would raise the political cost for the kidnapers of harming or killing them. There were no guarantees, we understood that. But it was an alternative to blind panic or paralysis.

Talking this over with John on the evening of December 1, an idea surfaced: what about creating a website and an online petition for their release? John is an experienced webweaver, and such is the accessibility of the internet that within two hours, *www.freethecaptivesnow.org* was up and running, with a petition and links to public statements calling for the release of the four captives.

For the first several days of December, there was a

growing international chorus of such statements, even from very militant Muslim groups, supporting the CPT workers and their release. Our online petition, along with another, soon gathered more than 50,000 signatures from around the world. There were vigils and rallies. While we were terrified for our friends, the swelling response made this an exciting period.

But after December 8, when the second deadline for executing Tom and the others passed, momentum shifted. The flurry of statements died down; news reports dwindled and became routine; and from Baghdad there was ominous silence about our friends, amid the noise and cries of civil war. For John and me, at our website, frantic effort to beat a deadline was replaced by keeping a vigil.

Every night of those thirteen weeks, either he or I would scan dozens of wire service reports for news of Tom and the others, and post what we found: with only a few exceptions, the news was "no news." The exceptions were when the gloomy videos of the four – and then, on March 7, 2006 the three, minus Tom – were released. On March 10 came the dispatch we dreaded most: confirmation of Tom's murder. (Early reports that he had been tortured were not confirmed by a later autopsy.) The only relief from this loss appeared on March 23, when the other three captives were freed.

Who killed Tom? And why? Few other than the ones who pulled the trigger know the truth, and one wonders how much even they understand. Speculation abounds, of course, with many of my more left-leaning friends imagining a CIA-sponsored conspiracy to silence these noisy pacifist dissenters. Yet from the reading and interviews I have done, however, the most likely guess seems much more mundanely sordid: it was all about money.

The videos showing Tom and the others were issued by a previously unknown group, "the Swords of Righteousness Brigades." This name is very likely a fake, a cover for a criminal gang, which simply kidnaped them for ransom. There is, as John and I learned while keeping our vigil, a sizeable kidnaping industry in Iraq. Many Iraqis have been thus abducted for profit, as well as citizens of numerous other countries.

James Loney felt the ransom was wanted to help finance the guerilla insurgency. Many other observers feel that while the kidnapers are Muslims, and many have likely suffered from the invasion and occupation, these crimes appear to be only loosely connected to religious or political grievances. Rather, they are more a specimen of organized crime in a devastated and lawless society.

From this "profit-seeking" perspective, taking CPT team members was not a particularly good "investment": the group has pledged not to pay, and not to ask anyone else to. Moreover, none of the four had a personal fortune to plunder. But the gang likely figured that regardless of such brave declarations, given enough pressure, someone would eventually cave in and pay. (Harmeet Sooden later told a New Zealand press conference that he suspected a ransom had been paid for him and the other survivors, despite vehement government denials.)

But if the kidnapers were after money, why kill Tom? There are a number of hypotheses:

One, to show the friends and supporters of the other three that the kidnapers meant business. Some other hostage killings – for instance, that of longtime relief worker Margaret Hassan, an Iraqi citizen originally from Ireland – were evidently staged to show recalcitrant governments that ransom demands were life and death matters.

Or two: because Tom was an American, and as a veteran had a US military ID card, he was a certified "enemy," and one for whom the US government would not pay. That made him worthled and disposable.

Or three: if the kidnapers couldn't get ransom from Tom's family or government, maybe they recouped something by selling Tom to another Iraqi insurgent gang, one willing to pay for the privilege of shooting a military-identified American. (It is all-too easy to imagine their derision at his protests that he was a musician, not a fighter.)

Again, no one knows, but these are plausible explanations for the inexplicable.

With Tom's death and the freeing of Jim Loney, Norman Kember and Harmeet Sooden, our *www.freethecaptivesnow.org* website morphed into a memorial and an archive, and we wound up our nightly vigil. I felt more than a little guilty about moving on, as the daily discipline of focusing on Iraq's ongoing agony had brought home in cruel detail how many thousands more men and women there were being kidnaped, held, tortured, and some killed, by factions from all sides, amid a bloody confusion of agendas.

With Tom gone, and the other CPTers free, I was

xiii

abandoning these legions, to return to some semblance of everyday routine. In truth, I can only hang my head and cite the Qur'an , Surra 4:110: "And whoever does evil or wrongs himself but afterwards seeks Allah's forgiveness, he will find Allah Oft-forgiving, Most merciful."

III

Yet Tom's story does not stop there. In the founding saga from which his CPT team took its marching orders, death was a tragedy, but not the end of the drama. Further, Tom was a Quaker, and in this tradition "be patterns, be examples," and "let your life preach" are among our oldest and most venerable mandates." Moreover, in our yearly meeting, my role has recently been in the religious education end, particularly with adults.

Thus while this small book is a memorial and a tribute, it is meant primarily for study and reflection. Rather, it attempts to follow these Friendly injunctions, and continue Tom's story as a well of patterns and examples. I believe he would recognize and approve such a project. Indeed, for the epigraph of his blog-journal, Tom used a paraphrase of the quote from which these mottos are taken.

Thus in the following pages, various persons reflect on passages from Tom's writings, or their memories and impressions of him, and offer comments on the patterns and examples of this remarkable, foreshortened life.

The views and affiliations here are diverse, and a few entries are unfriendly, even harsh. The latter were included because what they express is also part of the story, and the teaching. But hearing and learning even from the scoffers is part of our calling. Easy or not, everything here is meant as a prod to this process which is as religious as it is pedagogical. Tom alluded to this in a sermon to a Mennonite congregation between trips to the Middle East: "We did a lot of listening in Iraq with CPT, and the stories we heard were not always easy to hear."

'Walk cheerfully" is another Quaker motto. Tom was naturally cheerful. But even he had to struggle to maintain this outlook in Iraq. On August 30, 2005 he was struck by a quote from Elizabeth Blackwell: "I must have something in life which will fill this vacuum and prevent this sad wearing away of the heart."

"This was the quote today in my planner," Tom wrote, "as

I considered the tragedies both great and small, personal and global we are all dealing with. . . . The only 'something in my life' I can hold onto is to do what little I can to bring about the creation of the Peaceable Realm of God. It is my sense that such a realm will always have natural disasters. It is the 'man-made' disasters that we are called upon to bring to an end."

Tom sought to hold on to hope wherever he was. This was a difficult task in the regions where he chose to work. Of one rare encouraging incident, in Palestine, he recalled, "Here was a seed that can take root. Here were people working through their anger and coming out the other side committed to peace. Here were people listening to their hearts and listening to each other. Here a tiny part of the Peaceable Realm was created. Here was the justice of God taking shape."

Can that also happen here?

– Chuck Fager,
Quaker House
Fayetteville North Carolina

1. From James Loney

Easter 2006

For 118 days we lay in a tomb – Norman Kember, Harmeet Sooden and me. Tom Fox too, for 104 days, until he was murdered in the early morning hours of March 9.

Our tomb was a 10-ft.-by-10-ft. room. How I came to hate every single detail of it: the
paint-peeling walls; the dim light filtered through stained bedsheet "curtains"; the pebble-speckle pattern of the floor tiles; the never-ending hours and days of sitting, sleeping, three-times-a-day eating, handcuffed and chained except when let free to go to the bathroom . . . .

The captors wanted money to fund their war against the occupation of Iraq. If ransom was negotiated, it would be young American soldiers who paid. If ransom was denied – the policy of both the Canadian government and Christian Peacemaker Teams, the organization I work for – it would be one or all of us hostages who paid. If an attempt was made to rescue us by force, it would be a soldier or a captor or one of us that paid.

Even if our captors decided to just let us go, clearly the best possible scenario, there was still the cost of losing face, something I sensed they were not prepared to do. In the end, it was Tom who paid.. . . .

I am learning many things from my captivity, and have a universe of things to be grateful for. Among them is a new and deep appreciation for the women and men who wear the uniform of military service. I likely would not be writing this today if it were not for them. Thus, I am confronted with a great paradox. I, the Christian pacifist peacemaker, am alive, am free because of the very institutions I believe are contrary to Christian teaching. . . .

I'm learning that there are many kinds of prisons and many kinds of tombs. Prisons of the mind, the heart, the body. Tombs of despair, fear, confusion. Tombs within tombs and prisons within prisons.

1

There are no easy answers. We must all find our way through a broken world, struggling with the paradox of call and failure. My captivity and rescue have helped me to catch a glimpse of how powerful the force of resurrection is. Christ, that tomb-busting suffering servant Son of God, seeks us wherever we are, reaches for us in whatever darkness we inhabit.

May we reach for each other with that same persistence. The tomb is not the final word.

Jeremy Hinzman

When I first heard the news that four Christian Peacemaker Team volunteers had been taken hostage in Iraq, my first reaction was one of anger. I happened to have an acquaintance with Jim Loney. Before dawn on Easter of 2005, during the time that we celebrate the miracle of the risen Christ, he and I rode our bicycles out to a panoramic point on Lake Ontario. We welcomed the coming of a new day. There we joined other friends and Catholic Workers, and danced until the sun rose.

I was angry because I knew one of the captives, and know him to be a person who was pure of heart. This anger I mention coincides with that of all of us in the resistance here in Canada. We are fed up with the power that is in our midst. I am fed up today because the Tom Fox blog entries I was to use in order to get to know him better are not on my hard drive now, as they were this morning at the internet cafe.

Is all of this as mystifying to you as it is to me? The power that we all tirelessly work so hard to defeat has, I'm afraid, gone cellular. Perhaps I feel defensive, and depressed. But I'm not going to give up. The force of light will outshine the dark of imperialistic arrogance when everything comes to an end. I hope Tom had this faith too. I hope he still does.

We Canadians are a lazy bunch. From what little I know about Tom, I know he was definitely American, an activist in his witness. Is this why he was killed and the others spared? Although I too am susceptible to laying the problems of the world on Islamicism, blaming Muslims for Tom's death just seems like too easy of an answer. Tom knew there are hard choices we must make for the work of peace.

2

Hopefully, none of us want to be martyrs. Being a symbol, though, is something that, whether one lives or dies, one must embrace. However, if we are to be symbols, we must always remember to do it in the spirit of the early church. As I understand it, the spirit of the apostles and their community was centered on giving without the expectation of return. For in order to return to our true home, we must always be willing to go a distance. And what distance is that?

Running marathons is not a sport foreign to me. It was something I always wanted to do when I was a young American. Since I have moved to Canada, I have run three marathons, and one ultra-marathon, which was fifty kilometers. And what did I learn from running these marathons?

Perseverance may not always be enough. What we need to do in order to survive as a people is to love one another as Christ loved his enemies. Tom Fox loved the Iraqi people as he loved his fellow Christian peacemakers. Tom epitomized the Christ-like spirit of giving that we all must hope for if we want to be redeemed.

Jeremy Hinzman grew up in South Dakota, and joined the army after September 11, 2001. While assigned as a paratrooper to the 82d Airborne Division at Ft. Bragg, North Carolina, he filed a claim seeking noncombatant status as a conscientious objector. His claim was unsuccessful, but while it was pending he served several months in Afghanistan. Several months after his return from Afghanistan, his unit received orders for Iraq. Instead, in December 2003 Jeremy, his wife and young son went to Toronto, Canada. Their application for refugee status there remains unresolved as of this writing, in May 2006.

Suggested readings:

Leonard Desroches, *Allow the Water,* Dunamis Press.
Edward Said, *Culture & Imperialism*, Vintage.
David S. Reynolds, *John Brown, Abolitionist*, Knopf.
The Rivers North of the Future: The Testament of Ivan Illich, as told to David Cayley. House of Anansi.

2. Remembering Margaret Hassan

Tom – Monday, November 15, 2004

"Giving material goods can help people. If food is needed and we can give it, we do that. If shelter is needed, or books or medicine is needed, and we can give them, we do that. As best we can, we can care for whoever needs our care. Nevertheless, the real transformation takes place when we let go of our attachments and give away what we think we can't."
— When Things Fall Apart *by Pema Chodron*

Margaret Hassan* lived a life of giving away what we think we can't. She came to Iraq more than thirty years ago, a foreigner in a land that has been manipulated and oppressed by foreigners for much of the last millennium. Yet she came and lived with the people and grew to love them so much that she became a citizen.

She lived a life of giving away the human need for security. She worked tirelessly for the people of Iraq, coping with governments whose human rights record varied from somewhat intolerant to outright oppressive. She lived a life with the people of Iraq, not a life spent behind gates and walls.

Finally it seems as if she gave away her life. Individuals who resort to any means in order to justify their ends appear to have taken it from her. The Christian Peacemaker Team (CPT) in Iraq prays that these individuals can reconnect with their humanity. We pray for healing for her family, friends and co-workers. We understand that the Qu'ran teaches that an innocent person who is killed travels as quickly as does light to the gates of Paradise.

While Margaret's light may now be in Paradise her physical presence is no longer with the people of Iraq. We ask all people who have lived in her light and all who seek the light to resolve to continue the work she began. She lived a life of courage in the midst of fear. We are called to do the same, no matter what

4

the consequences.

CPT has had the privilege of knowing Margaret during the two years that CPT has been in Iraq. She met with a number of visiting delegations and shared with them her vision for the future of her country. One CPT member reflected on his experiences with her, "Margaret and her staff placed their energies into building the future for the people of Iraq. When attackers bombed their warehouse last year, they moved the operation, but continued their efforts with other Iraqis to improving life in this country. Margaret modeled an extravagant way of living for others."

* Margaret Hassan (1945-2004) an born in Ireland and married to an Iaqi. She had lived in Iraq for many years, gained Iraqi citizenship, and had worked with CARE there since 1991. Fluent in Arabic, and a vocal opponent of the US invasion of Iraq, she was kidnaped in October of 2004, and apparently murdered several weeks later.

Unobstructed Love

The problem with unobstructed love is that it's rarely understood. Maybe that s because it does not appear like any other love – puppy love, romantic love, true love, love of country. No, unobstructed love is unlike anything we see in day-to-day life. It is seen mostly in stories of great heroes.

But even then it's so rarely witnessed that it can seem illogical, perhaps even a sickness or a chronic miscalculation.

But when the Light shines through one's soul and there becomes a certainty of what one must do, even after all the tantrums of asking that the cup pass from our lips, and the horizon one sees is suddenly more broad then ever before – well, it's not easily forgotten. The rare gift to be one with one's word, hopes, and faith washes up a dingy day and a mangy life to a spit shine inwardly and outwardly. It holds all of creation within reach of understanding and just far enough away to remain in awe.

The surrender does not come easy as it is non-verbal and lacks explanation. Whether it is a visitation, a message, or a simple knowing, the experience is a private one and known in one's heart and deep in the gut. How we shall think about it or which words to use comes about later with time and wonder and our awkward attempts to make sense of another realm.

When love has the walls around it lifted so that care and compassion are moved up and out of the rat runs of ordinary living, the transformation resembles water seeking its own level. The rules of gravity have been changed and it might be that there is no downhill and yet there is great motion and new movement and expanse.

We are spotty in our practice of unobstructed love. We try to love the ones we know we should. We might even try to love the ones we did love before something came undone. There's the duty to love the inferior and goodness knows there's slews of them. But what of loving all that is? What of loving those who might do us great harm, perhaps the ultimate harm? Could Jesus possibly have meant to Love our enemies? Surely, it's metaphor or a translation problem.

And yet, at the stage of unobstructed love, it's a simple reach. Not a simple practice, goodness knows, but once glimpsed, the temptation to feel and see that Grace again is too wondrous to await chance. No, this is an elixir beyond all.

And so it comes that a Mother Teresa, a Martin King, a Daniel Berrigan, a Gandhi set off on some spiritual adventure and the great parade of spectators haven't a clue as to the core of the adventure, not a clue–not want house and car, leave family and home, be in danger–maybe in jail or war zone? How could this not appear as madness for the merely in love?

The moments of Grace are not so rare. But the signing up for the life-time subscription and heeding the call, that's when the crowd thins out. For the blessed few who reach that state of love and stay on, it's a ride that teaches us all how limited our vision is and how regular our hopes. This is not a ride for anyone. There's no gift in being misunderstood by so many.

No, this is a ride for a few and a message to us all that great love exists and can change hearts, move mountains and empires, and provide an edge to the known world for us to wonder at and hope the blessing comes again soon to someone.

John Calvi, from Putney Vermont, is the convener of The Quaker Initiative to End Torture. He has been working with torture survivors since 1982 as a Quaker healer and massage therapist.

6

3. *"What Does That Mean – 'Tame'?*

Tom – Friday, October 22, 2004

. . . When I allow myself to become angry I disconnect from God and connect with the evil force that empowers fighting. When I allow myself to become fearful I disconnect from God and connect with the evil force that encourages flight. I take Gandhi and Jesus at their word--if I am not one with God then I am one with Satan. I don't think Gandhi would use that word but Jesus certainly did, on numerous occasions. The French theologian René Girard has a very powerful vision of Satan that speaks to me: "Satan sustains himself as a parasite on what God creates by imitating God in a manner that is jealous, grotesque, perverse and as contrary as possible to the loving and obedient imitation of Jesus" (I Saw Satan Fall Like Lighting, *R. Girard, pg. 45).*

If I am not to fight or flee in the face of armed aggression, be it the overt aggression of the army or the subversive aggression of the terrorist, then what am I to do? "Stand firm against evil" (Matthew 5:39, translated by Walter Wink) seems to be the guidance of Jesus and Gandhi in order to stay connected with God. But here in Iraq I struggle with that second form of aggression. I have visual references and written models of CPTers standing firm against the overt aggression of an army, be it regular or paramilitary. But how do you stand firm against a car--bomber or a kidnapper? Clearly the soldier being disconnected from God needs to have me fight. Just as clearly the terrorist being disconnected from God needs to have me flee. Both are willing to kill me using different means to achieve the same end. That end being to increase the parasitic power of Satan within God's good creation.

It seems easier somehow to confront anger within my heart

7

than it is to confront fear. But if Jesus and Gandhi are right then I am not to give in to either. I am to stand firm against the kidnapper as I am to stand firm against the soldier. Does that mean I walk into a raging battle to confront the soldiers? Does that mean I walk the streets of Baghdad with a sign saying "American for the Taking"? No to both counts. But if Jesus and Gandhi are right, then I am asked to risk my life and if I lose it to be as forgiving as they were when murdered by the forces of Satan. I struggle to stand firm but I'm willing to keep working at it.

John Stephens

"What does that mean – 'tame'?"

"It is an act too often neglected," said the fox. "It means to establish ties."

"'To establish ties'?"

"Just that," said the fox. "To me, you are still nothing more than a little boy who is just like a hundred thousand other little boys. And I have no need of you. And you, on your part, have no need of me. To you, I am nothing more than a fox like a hundred thousand other foxes. But if you tame me, then we shall need each other. To me, you will be unique in all the world. To you, I shall be unique in all the world . . ."

– from *The Little Prince* by Antoine de Saint-Exupéry (68)

Fox, Girard, & The Little Prince

I met Tom Fox at the natural foods grocery store where we both worked before he retired in 2003. When I worked with him, he had served the company for nearly a decade as a baker, a bakery team leader, and associate store team leader. At that time I had no reason to think he would be anything more than a boss like a hundred thousand other bosses.

But over the course of our time together he shared with me concrete disciplines for putting first things first, living simply, and serving others. In time I realized he was a mentor to me, and he made me his friend. We shared bread, we hiked together, and as Quakers, we shared clear silences and reflected on the practical challenges facing our faith and community in a culture of war and terror.

I have heard a great number of people interpret Tom's story as an expression of ideology or political agenda. Those stories may be important parts of Tom's impact on our lives, but they have nothing to do with the Tom Fox I know. What Tom shared with me, and many others who knew him, was something that often disappears when the conversation shifts to ideology and politics, something that I can only call Communion.

The communion I learned from Tom is what Jim Corbett calls "'religio,' a 'rebinding' into open society [that is] the distinctively human form of sociality and civility" (Corbett 106). In practical terms, this is about sharing meals and fellowship, or as Saint-Exupéry's fox said so aptly "establishing ties." If there is a single quality that unites Tom's work and witness in all of the communities he served, it was that he brought people together to share bread and establish ties of fellowship. I cannot help but imagine that this was the original meaning of the Eucharist for the early Church, as expressed in the letters of Paul and the Didache, an early Christian "handbook."

But Tom was also concerned about a great breakdown of communion that demoralizes human life in society. He spoke about this only with great humility and bewilderment, but I later found out that he had been struggling with this issue for many, many years.

I am a member of Woodlawn Friends Meeting, which is the community where Tom's family came to the Quaker faith over twenty years ago. Our meetinghouse was built by the family of Quaker Chalkley Gillingham before the American Civil War. During that war, the meetinghouse was "pressed into service" as an infirmary and military headquarters (even while Friends continued to worship there), and Quakers "lost their crops, livestock, fences, barns, and houses to marauding soldiers from both armies" (Nations).

Like many Quakers, Gillingham kept a journal, much of which recounts the wartime trials this small Quaker community endured. Tom found an unpublished copy, and was drawn to it. He devoted a lot of attention and study to this period, and headed a committee to transcribe, edit, and publish Gillingham's journal. Through this work, Tom traced the chronicles of violent contagion that surrounded this "Friend in the midst of Civil War." It is now evident that for Tom, this work wasn't a matter of idle curiosity,

9

but a meaningful study into one of the most significant challenges facing Friends today. It was a practical concern.

The scope and nature of this challenge came into even clearer focus during Tom's deployment with Christian Peacemaker Teams in Iraq. In the blog that he began after he arrived in Baghdad, Tom included the word "Satan" in his vocabulary, a concept he'd never spoken about in our prior conversations, and one that I'd never taken seriously. "This force of war," he said "... leads a person, or country, or ethnic group to walk away from God and towards the contagion of Satan." [Emphasis mine.] The way he inflected the term seemed unique, but it remained a mystery until later.

After Tom's death, I was given many of his books. Among these, the one with the most highlighter marks and notes was *I Saw Satan Fall Like Lightning* by René Girard.

As I began to read it, the parallels to the situation at hand seemed uncanny, even unnerving. Girard writes as an anthropologist, and his central focus in this text is the breakdown of communion that gives rise to menace, war, and terror in every age. He dispassionately describes a process whereby imitation of desire becomes rivalry, and rivalry becomes virulent throughout human society. At its crescendo, when rivalistic contagion must erupt into violence from which no one is safe, the process creates a single victim for the community to slay or exile as a scapegoat.

The Passion of the Christ, according to Girard, is a single lucid example of this process, and it seems that the murder of my friend Tom, amid countless others killed in Iraq, is another. Violent tension explodes out of infectious rivalry, triggering the need for a sacrifice. Because the process almost always yields a single victim for the community to demonize and accuse, Girard calls the process Satanic: "The devil, or Satan, signifies rivalistic contagion, up to and including the single victim mechanism. He may be located in the entire process or in one of its stages" (Girard 43). [Emphasis mine.]

But why doesn't Satan present himself as an impersonal principle ... ? Because he designates the principal consequence of the single victim mechanism, the emergence of a false transcendence and the numerous deities that represent it. Satan is always someone. (Girard 46) [Emphasis in original.]

That last sentence was highlighted by Tom in the text: Satan is always someone. When violent contagion has the whole community in its grip, someone must be accused, someone must be taken down, someone must be lynched, someone must be killed, someone must serve as a focus for the community's hostility – or else the community will annihilate itself. A fleeting sense of relief from the snowballing of rivalries only arises when the community unites in the sacrifice of a single victim.

Tom's colleagues in CPT attest that he thought heavily on these subjects; Norman Kember mentioned that during their Bible study sessions in captivity, Tom shared a great deal from his reflections on Girard. But no one I've talked with really knows what Tom made of this study, and perhaps we never will. Recalling that Tom's life was taken in events that morbidly illustrate Girard's thesis makes the concept that much more difficult to get my head around.

What I know of Tom, and I can practice in my own life, is building communion. As a thoroughly flawed human being in a community divided by politics, ideology, wealth, and privilege, my way is difficult, and averting apocalyptic tension seems hopeless. But my struggle with Tom's legacy is defined by communion and service: sharing bread and establishing meaningful ties of fellowship where fellowship is strained by mistrust, menace, war, and terror. Establishing the Peaceable Realm of God, as Tom put it, means loving, serving, and healing my neighbor through real human contact.

Communion is more than a passive undertaking; it can be an active resistance to the contagion of Satan. As a community practice, communion may erode the foundation of rivalistic tension and redeem real people from dehumanizing and demonizing others. Perhaps that is too much to hope. As a covenant I inherit from a cherished Friend, the difficult practice of taming and being tamed reminds me that I am still the learner, and the Fox is still my teacher.

"Men have forgotten this truth," said the fox. "But you must not forget it. You become responsible, forever, for what you have tamed" (Saint-Exupéry 74).

Sources & Further Reading
Citations of René Girard in the above text refer to *I Saw Satan Fall Like Lightning,* below.
Buckman, Christine, Christy DeButts, and Tom Fox eds. "The

11

Journal of Chalkley Gillingham: Friend in the Midst of Civil War."
Fort Belvior: Alexandria Friends Meeting at Woodlawn, 1989.
(The publication date is given in note 15 on page 38.)

Corbett, Jim. *Goatwalking: A Guide to Wildland Living, a Quest for the Peaceable Kingdom.* New York: Viking, 1991.

Erhman, Bart D. *The New Testament and Other Early Christian Writings: A Reader.* New York: Oxford UP, 1998.

Fox, Tom. "The Force of War and the Force of Peace? The Same Force Moving in the Opposite Direction?" *Waiting in the Light.* 14 Feb 2005.

http://waitinginthelight.blogspot.com/2005/02/force-of-war-and-force-of-peace-same.html

Girard, René, and Yvonne Fraccero trans. *The Scapegoat.* Baltimore: Johns Hopkins University Press, 1986.

Girard, René, and James G. Williams trans. *I Saw Satan Fall Like Lightning.* Maryknoll: Orbis, 2002.

Nations, James. "Short History of Woodlawn Meeting." Alexandria Friends Meeting at Woodlawn. 7 Jan 2005. http://woodlawnfriends.org/home/?page_id=5

Saint-Exupéry, Antoine de and Katherine Woods trans. *The Little Prince.* New York: Harcourt, 1971.

4. Throwing Open the Book

Tom – Monday, February 14, 2005

. . . Perhaps the most difficult aspect of this peace energy would be a unified vision of the Peaceable Realm. We seem to have such a huge range of vision on relatively mundane things like what form of worship we participate in. Yet throughout the Hebrew scriptures as well as the Christian scripture (and the Buddhist and Taoist and yes even a good part of the Muslim sacred writings) there is a unified vision. Both Isaiah and Jesus used the metaphor of the "the way" as did Buddha and Lao Tzu. Mohammed spoke of the "straight path." Are they all talking about the direction the force of peace sends us that brings us to a true relationship with God?

Thursday, May 12, 2005

It was the 20th of April, the birthday of the prophet Mohammed. We had guests from Najaf and Kerbala visiting us for dinner that night. For grace before the meal a CPTer went into the office and opened up the team's English/Arabic Qu'ran and put his finger down on this passage,

"One day shalt thou see the believing men and the believing women–how their Light runs forward before them. And by their right hands their greeting will be, 'Good News for you this Day! Gardens beneath which flow rivers! To dwell therein for you! This indeed is the highest achievement."
– Surra 40 " God Most Gracious" section 2, verse 12

We asked one of our guests to recite it in Arabic and then a CPTer would read the English translation. It was a passage the guest knew from memory. This opened up a discussion of the tradition in Islam, Christianity and Judaism of throwing open the holy book of that faith tradition and reading the first passage that your eyes fall upon. Is this superstition? Does it have any

13

relevance for our broken lives and chaotic world?

Many people have said that there is no logical, rational reason for CPT to be in Iraq right now. The level of violence, which subsided after the elections, has risen each week until now the attacks and kidnappings of Iraqi officials, civilians and internationals are as bad or worse than the months leading up to the election . . . .

Why is CPT here when the "principalities and powers" seem to be in total control? What can a few (currently three) of us do in the face of such massive physical and structural violence?

We are throwing ourselves open to the possibility of God's grace bringing some rays of light to the shadowy landscape that is Iraq. We are letting ourselves be guided by something that is beyond rational, intellectual analysis. Gardens beneath which flow rivers can again be the dwelling place for the people of Iraq.

Everyone whose government and corporations are playing a role in this land needs to throw open the book of their heart. They need to let their Light run before them as they bring redemption to those in power who are seeking to rule from a place of fear, violence and shadows. That truly would be the highest achievement.

From the Qur'an:

2:155-156: And certainly, we shall test you with something of fear; hunger; loss of wealth, lives and fruits, but give glad tidings to the patient ones, who, when afflicted with calamity say, 'Truly! To Allah we belong and truly, to Him we shall return."

2:216; It may be that you dislike a thing which is good for you and that you like a thing which is bad for you. Allah knows but you do not know.

3:140: If a wound [and killing] has touched you, be sure a similar wound [and killing] has touched the others.

3:145: And no person can ever die except by Allah's leave and at an appointed term.

4:110: And whoever does evil or wrongs himself but afterwards seeks Allah's forgiveness, he will find Allah Oft-forgiving, Most merciful.

5:82: And you will find the nearest in love to the believers, those who say: "We are Christians."

13:11: For each [person] there are angels in succession, before and behind him. They guard him by the Command of Allah.

13:24: Peace be upon you, because you persevered in patience! Excellent indeed is the final home!

14:34: And if you could count the graces of Allah, never could you be able to count them.

16:127: And endure you patiently, your patience is not but from Allah.

25:63: The worshipers of the All-Merciful are they who tread gently upon the earth, and when the ignorant address them, they reply, "Peace!"

41:34: repel that which is evil with one which is better, then verily! He, between whom and you there was enmity, [will become] as though he was a close friend.

42:28: And he is it Who sends down the rain after they have despaired, and spreads abroad His Mercy.

42:40: But whoever forgives and makes reconciliation, his

15

reward is due from Allah.

76:9; We feed you seeking Allah's Countenance only. We wish for no reward, nor thanks from you.

Sayings of Muhammad (Hadith):

"Verily, Allah ordered me to keep relations with those that cut me off, to forgive the one who does an injustice with me, and to give to those who withhold from me."

"Love the one who is beloved to you in due moderation, for perhaps the day will come when you will abhor him. And hate the one whom you detest in due moderation, for perhaps the day will arrive when you will come to love him."

Reflection by Khalilah Sabra

John Dryden once said,

"Our souls sit close and silently within,

And their own webs from their own entrails spin."

The freedom fighter lives within the web consisting of a central point that might be accurately described as humanity, the spiritual base and signet of his sacred ideology. However, the weaved web may trap what has become its prey, even if it offers no element of danger. Its prey may be actually offering what is beneficial and good. But in the end, with all his good intentions, he was subjected to the whims and desires of the elements. Tom Fox became the prey and fell to the unholy desires of the elements.

There is a saying in Islam, "The pen has been lifted and the pages are dry." Could Tom Fox have avoided his appointment with the angels? I do not believe so. Our lives here are apportioned, but the manner in which we die is significant. There are moments in life when to do the wise thing is, in fact, to take the most difficult stance possible. Here was a man with a calling, a resolute tune fraught with danger and jeopardy, yet he allowed the force of his goodness to speed him in that direction. He sought to sedate the agents of death and despair in Iraq, whose crimes have been

16

committed with an ice like alienation from the destruction that they create, from the agonies that they empowered and the harm that has no end in sight. This is a huge undertaking for any peacemaker who comes into these sorts of situations, initially at least, with a degree of trust that good shall overcome evil. The way the power structure kills that sense of trust is cumulative, rough at the roots, consciously intended and in some cases, physically annihilating.

Unfortunately, Tom's life was ended by those he tried to help–but for every action there is a reaction, and with no intention to humanize or validate his murderers, the occupier of Iraq must take his share of the blame. As an optimist, Tom Fox, humbly attempted to manipulate the odds, they, however, went against his favor.

Some might say that he died in vain, unable to deflect an unyielding and sophisticate social order, but I do not think so. It was his choice not to hold back and he sat an example for others. He knew that he could not aspire to do the things he did without paying a serious price and it is his actions that should teach us. If we hope to truly change the world, we too will also have to pay the price. We may lose our careers, relationships and like Tom, even our lives. In the long run this is what change demands.

An American convert to Islam, Khalilah Sabra pursued criminal justice and paralegal studies at California State University, Los Angeles and her graduate work in Paralegal Studies at UCLA. She has lived in Lebanon and worked with refugees in Afghanistan. She is co-host of a TV program for the Muslim American Public Affairs Council of North Carolina.

5. Fight or Flight?

Tom – Friday, October 22, 2004

"If an attacker inspires anger or fear in my heart, it means that I have not purged myself of violence. To realize nonviolence means to feel within you its strength–soul force–to know God. A person who has known God will be incapable of harboring anger or fear within him [or her], no matter how overpowering the cause for that anger or fear may be."

(Gandhi speaking to Badshah Kahn's Khudai Khidmatgar officers; A Man to Match His Mountains, *by Eknath Easwaran.)*

*When I allow myself to become angry I disconnect from God and connect with the evil force that empowers fighting. When I allow myself to become fearful I disconnect from God and connect with the evil force that encourages flight. I take Gandhi and Jesus at their word--if I am not one with God then I am one with Satan. I don't think Gandhi would use that word but Jesus certainly did, on numerous occasions. The French theologian René Girard has a very powerful vision of Satan that speaks to me: "Satan sustains himself as a parasite on what God creates by imitating God in a manner that is jealous, grotesque, perverse and as contrary as possible to the loving and obedient imitation of Jesus" (*I Saw Satan Fall Like Lighting, *R. Girard).*

If I am not to fight or flee in the face of armed aggression, be it the overt aggression of the army or the subversive aggression of the terrorist, then what am I to do? "Stand firm against evil" (Matthew 5:39, translated by Walter Wink) seems to be the guidance of Jesus and Gandhi in order to stay connected with God. But here in Iraq I struggle with that second form of aggression. I have visual references and written models of CPTers standing firm against the overt aggression of an army, be it regular or paramilitary. But how do you stand firm against a car-bomber or a kidnapper? Clearly the soldier being disconnected from God needs to have me fight. Just as clearly the terrorist being disconnected from God needs to have me flee. Both are willing to kill me using different means to achieve the same end. That end being to increase the parasitic power of Satan within God's good creation.

It seems easier somehow to confront anger within my heart than it is to confront fear. But if Jesus and Gandhi are right then I am not to give in to either. I am to stand firm against the kidnapper as I am to stand firm against the soldier.

Does that mean I walk into a raging battle to confront the soldiers? Does that mean I walk the streets of Baghdad with a sign saying "American for the Taking"? No to both counts. But if Jesus and Gandhi are right, then I am asked to risk my life and if I lose it to be as forgiving as they were when murdered by the forces of Satan. I struggle to stand firm but I'm willing to keep working at it.

Tribute to Tom Fox by Swami Shraddhananda

It is no wonder that Tom Fox studied Mahatma Gandhi's words and drew inspiration from his writings. Tom practiced yoga and studied/lived/promoted peace. For thousands of years human beings have used non-violent means to build civilizations, settle conflicts, and sustain life in families, communities, nations. However, it was not until Mahatma Gandhi applied the yogic spiritual principle of Ahimsa (non-violence) to the struggle against British imperialism and occupation that the world recognized the power of peace to bring massive social change.

The strategy and tactics of non-violence on a conscious, public, and mass scale have since then brought the overthrow of apartheid in South Africa, the victories of the Civil Rights era in the U.S., the ouster of the Marcos regime in the Philippines, and many, many other proofs of the power of non-violent action. Non-Cooperation with violence and cooperation with peace were hallmarks of both Gandhi and Tom Fox and millions of others who have participated/are participating in non-violent ways to speak truth to power.

The practice of non-violence is rooted in the deeply spiritual concept that recognizes the divine in all of creation, that encourages the unity of each individual with God-consciousness, and is based firmly on a love-based version of reality (rather than fear-based). Tom's writings address these issues eloquently. He acknowledged it was fear more than anger that he had to grapple with as well (like so many of us).

Non-violence as a philosophical and political tool to change the relations of power globally is still relatively new on the planet. Gandhi's victory in India came after decades of educating and organizing and the culmination of that work in the 1940s is not really so long ago.

It took a dozen years of the practice of non-violence in myriad ways to end the U.S. war in Vietnam. From religious people pouring blood at recruitment stations, to armed services personnel refusing to fight, to massive peace marches, to longshoremen refusing to load the bombs headed for Vietnam - all demonstrated the power of educating and organizing non-violent action.

Today we are moving forward with our understanding of the power of non-violence. We know the courage of Tom Fox to bear witness to deeply held spiritual convictions; we know we also need to study and be inspired by those who have walked the path of peace before us, as Tom did; we recognize that we must popularize the victories of non-violent action in a broader way; and we know that the days and years ahead will provide many opportunities to apply these lessons.

Americans are awakening to the fact that the use of violence not only causes suffering to the victims of violence but also brutalizes the perpetrators of violence. To stand silent as our tax dollars fund bombs that kill mostly civilians, to stand silent as our government condones torture, to stand silent as US soldiers return broken from what they did to others as much as what was done to them, is to corrupt the soul of our nation.

Gandhi said, "The task of non-violence is to rush into the

mouth of violence."

For the memory of Tom Fox and for all those who have given their lives for peace: let us resolve to train ourselves and train others in the strategy and tactics of non-violence; let us master the history of the victories of non-violence and share this hope of "soul-force" with others; let us ground ourselves in the spiritual power of peace. Let us not mistake the temporary for the permanent. Namaste.

Swami Shraddhananda is an ordained priest in the Kriya Yoga tradition and teaches several peace and justice courses at DePaul University, including the Gandhi Non-Violence Conference Course. Her email is: mdolan1149@aol.com

For Further Reading:

Legacy of Love: My Education in the Path of Nonviolence by Arun Gandhi. North Bay Books, El Sobriante CA 2003.

Mohandas Gandhi: Essential Writings by Father John Dear. Orbis Books NY 2005.

Waging Non-Violent Struggle: 20th Century Practice and 21st Century Potential by Gene Sharp. Porter Sargent Publishers/Extending Horizons Books NH 2005.

6. The Force of Peace

Tom – Monday, February 14, 2005

The force of peace would require a great deal of organization and teamwork. Imagine a moment if the United States government had the same number of people working abroad and at home in the Peace Corps and Americorps as are in the armed forces. And that would just create a degree of stasis. A balance point not really moving us in the direction of God, just keeping us from moving in the direction of the "commander of the spiritual powers of the air" (Eph. 2:1)

Perhaps the most difficult aspect of this peace energy would be a unified vision of the Peaceable Realm. We seem to have such a huge range of vision on relatively mundane things like what form of worship we participate in. Yet throughout the Hebrew scriptures as well as the Christian scripture (and the Buddhist and Taoist and yes even a good part of the Muslim sacred writings) there is a unified vision. Both Isaiah and Jesus used the metaphor of the "the way" as did Buddha and Lao Tzu. Mohammed spoke of the "straight path." Are they all talking about the direction the force of peace sends us that brings us to a true relationship with God?

Would it be possible to bring about the Peaceable Realm and still keep our unique modes of worship?

Georgia Fuller

Yes, Tom, we can keep our unique modes of worship. When your kidnappers aired the first tape of you, Jim, Harmeet, and Norman in early December 2005, my heart stopped. But so did the hearts of other Christians and Muslims around the world.

Your captors announced a date for your executions December 8, Baghdad time. Here in Virginia that was 4 pm on December 7 to 4 pm December 8. We gathered at Langley Hill Friends Meeting in the evening of December 7 for a 24-hour vigil. We held all of you in the Light including the men who had taken you captive.

The media didn't get it at first. They asked us about fear, anger, rescue, and retaliation. But people of faith got it. As I worshipped that evening, I experienced the Light around you widening and growing brighter. Christians everywhere were praying, but also imams from Iraq, Palestine, and Western countries were calling for your release. Palestinian children rallied for your freedom–carrying pictures of you playing music. The deadline was extended two days.

We went home at 4 pm on Thursday, December 8, ready to come back and do it all again. But we didn't have to do it by ourselves. Our friends at the nearby ADAMS mosque included you in their Friday-night prayers. Afterward, they broadcast appeals for your release in English and Arabic over U.S., British, and Middle-Eastern media. Tom, it was beautiful!

We returned to Langley Hill that evening where many kept the second 24-hour vigil. New support for you came from other Muslim leaders and organizations, including Hamas and Hezbollah. Groups that practice violence understood that peacemakers are blessed children of God (Matthew 5:9). The new deadline for your execution passed, your captors said nothing, but our hearts told us you were still alive.

Thus began our "Friday Night Interfaith Peace Vigils." Every week Quakers, mainstream Christians, Muslims, Sikhs, Bahais, Jews, and others gathered to pray and share our visions of peace. So yes, Tom, we can keep our unique modes of worship in the Peaceable Realm.

23

Jesus said that we should worship in Spirit and in Truth (John 4:23-24). Worship is a matter of the heart not geography or architecture. God's Spirit is a guest that fills our hearts and points us toward the Divine Life. Jesus told us, "The Spirit blows where it chooses." God's Spirit can't be bound by creed or practice.

Pilate asked, "What is Truth?" Truth is not a doctrine but a way of living toward God, the way Jesus lived. The straight path to God who is love is not the way of hate, oppression, and violence. As the prophet Micah summarized, we are "to do justice, and to love kindness, and to walk humbly with [our] God." (6:8)

The Peaceable Realm has many names. Isaiah said the "wolf shall live with the lamb, the leopard shall lie down with the kid and the lion shall eat straw like the ox." (11:6-7) Our Quaker forbearer, Edward Hicks, used this scripture for over 62 paintings called the "Peaceable Kingdom." Jesus announced the coming Kingdom of God or Kingdom of Heaven. But Tom, you and I have never liked exclusive language and Kingdom is both classist and sexist. So you speak of the Peaceable Realm and I speak of God's Reign of Justice and Peace. I had looked forward to arguing with you about why my translation is better.

Word came of your death during our Friday Night Vigil on March 10. I know your love and faithfulness are more powerful than the hatred of those who killed you, but I still cry. We didn't get everything we prayed for, but Jim, Harmeet, and Norman were freed two weeks later. Love has not yet conquered all, but Tom, your love has conquered a lot.

Georgia E. Fuller first met Tom Fox in 1990 at Alexandria Friends Meeting where they both taught scripture. Tom was excited about the Gnostic gospels. This is one of several areas where Georgia and Tom disagreed. As a feminist, Georgia thinks that Gnostic writings are interesting, but that their treatments of the physical-material world as unreal, secondary, or even evil is not "good news" for women. Eventually both Tom and Georgia became members of Langley Hill Friends Meeting. Georgia has a doctorate in sociolinguistics and cultural anthropology and a second master's degree in scripture, biblical languages, and theology. She teaches wherever Friends will have her, including Pendle Hill. Two of her Monday night lectures are on the Pendle Hill website, "Tell Me a Story of Faith and Practice" (May 20, 1996) and "Taking the Bible Seriously and Suspiciously" (November 20, 2000).

Suggested Reading:

Georgia Fuller, "Johannine Lessons in Community, Witness, and Power," in *The Bible, the Church and the Future of Friends*, ed. by Chuck Fager, Pendle Hill, 1996.

Georgia Fuller, "Reflections on Emmanuel for the 21st Century," in *New Voices, New Light*, ed. by Chuck Fager, Pendle Hill, 1995.

Walter Wink, *The Powers That Be*, Augsburg Fortress, c.1998 (paperback, Galilee/Doubleday, New York, 1999)

7. Tunnel Vision

Tom – Monday, June 06, 2005

*"Iraqis always seem to have lots of guns in their houses."
A U.S. Army colonel was making reference to how prevalent gun
ownership is in Iraq. We were meeting with him in his office in the
Green Zone. Draped across his high back chair was an ornate
leather holster with his service revolver.*

*"Our young technician can barely keep up with the
demand." The colonel described the work of a sergeant who is an
expert in constructing artificial limbs. The colonel said proudly
that no one in Iraq has the equipment or expertise that this young
man has. Yet there did not seem to be an acknowledgement of why
there is such a demand for artificial limbs in Iraq at this time.*

*"The Iraqi NGOs we work with have a lot of trouble
developing a level of trust between them." He noted that when his
office organizes a conference of NGOs in the Green Zone often
they don't want to follow the set agenda but need to express their
lack of trust for the U.S. military and for each other. Yet he failed
to mention the years of totalitarian rule by Saddam followed by
two years of anarchy, neither of which would tend to develop trust
in any institutions.*

*"All of us took a nine hour seminar on understanding Iraqi
culture when we got here a year ago." The colonel said his unit
would be going home at the end of the month after a year in Iraq.
As is the case with many U.S. military and civilians working in the
Green Zone, the colonel said he has never set foot on a street in
Baghdad. He has never been inside the home of an Iraqi family nor
has he seen any of the historical or cultural sites of the country.*

It would seem easy to characterize the colonel as hypocritical and bigoted. I am not the greatest judge of character but I kept having an image of him on the North Rim of the Grand Canyon holding up a tube from a roll of paper towels [to his eye] and describing what he saw. We are all finite creatures with a very limited field of vision. But what I do (and it is my sense that the colonel does this also) instead of opening up my field of vision to include things that I don't understand or agree with is to make my field of vision even narrower.

"Out of sight, out of mind" is an old saying that seems rather apt in this case. The colonel seemed very confident that the vision of the world he described was an accurate and complete one. And this was true. Within his extremely limited world-view, his vision was indeed clear. But what about the vast universe he was not seeing? What about the vast universe I'm not seeing? How do we all expand our vision to see things we don't want to see? How do we stop putting "out of sight" things we don't agree with? I wish I had an answer but I don't even know where to start.

An Email to the Tom Fox Memorial Page

From: Anonymous <anonymous-comment@blogger.com>

Date: Mar 25, 2006 10:33 PM

Subject: New comment on Tom Fox Memorial Page

Anonymous has left a new comment on your post "Tom Fox Memorial Page":

I was saddened to hear of Tom's death, and deeply regret that he was murdered by these Islamic extremists. However, I do not regret the war that liberated the people of Iraq, or the concurrent seizure of so many thousands of rounds of artillery and missile chemical munitions (WMD), and removal from power of the despot Saddam Hussein, who had used them against Kurdish children, and Iranians.

As a soldier, I know the falsehood of the accusation that we "dehumanize" the people of Iraq as a part of our operations there, or even that our daily operations are focused on taking lives, instead of improving them. What monsters you think we are – more than 130,000 Americans and many others who see the people of Iraq daily, trying to live as normal people might.

We are not.

How could it be that we would dehumanize them as we renovate their very hospitals and build their very roadways, and have restored their power, and have brought them water?

I have been in the Army now 25 years, and I have never seen any manual or any class or any process designed to dehumanize anyone – But I have seen us in Haiti, and in Kosovo, and in Bosnia, and now in Iraq, uniformly trying our best to bring hope, and bread, and yes, PEACE to many people. Do we fail? Yes, sometimes.

But what I have seen which has troubled me more, frankly, is the dehumanization of American soldiers by the very people we seek to protect. I have seen groundless attacks upon our forces by those who understand the necessity of national defense when they are logically pushed into admitting it – but who see themselves as strictly above doing any of that themselves.

Tom was rare, he put feet to his convictions and went to Iraq to do something. This stands him in a very [select] group, and is admirable.

But I must speak the truth and say, I take exception to the myopic reading of Scripture which seems to drive the CPT, and the ease with which they seem to dismiss the so-called martyrs of Islam who daily murder the people, meanwhile condemning Christians like me who bear arms in their defense (or in their rescue, as the case may dictate).

It may not seem as glorious, but there is another duty, and it is also Christian. That duty is to find out what God wants, and then to do it. I accomplish that by reading the Bible and through prayer.

It is as if CPT never heard of Jesus turning over the tables in the Temple and driving out the money changers with a whip.[Matthew 21:12-13; John 2:13-16]

It is as if nobody at CPT ever read how Jesus admonished his disciples to sell their garments and to buy swords in Luke 22 -- they said they had two, and He said it was enough. Two in twelve men armed with swords would give us an Army much smaller by percentage than that of Joshua's Israel, but it would still be twenty-five million strong – fifty times its current size.

Did Jesus instruct them to sin? Did he ask them to purchase swords knowing that such was evil? I do not think so.

Turn the other cheek in my own behalf, yes.[Matthew 5:38-39] I will. Disregard the defense of my children (and yours) from such as would execute a man for his conversion to Christ? I can not do it and be true to my Christian duty.

And so, thank God the others are free – but Tom's accusation of dehumanizing, or that the kidnappings were the fault of those who freed Iraq, and those who continue to stand alongside its new government – I can not forget that, and I will not stand silently as people continue to misrepresent them.

From the Al-Aqsa Martyrs Brigade

December 4, 2005

From your brothers in arms, the sons of the same blood who have suffered from one enemy, to the fighters against the invaders in Iraq, at a time when we are engaged in one battle against a single unjust plan by Zionist imperialism; a plan aimed at dividing the region, the theft of its wealth and the subduing of its peoples in the name of deceitful excuses such as the spreading of democracy and freedom, we appeal to the hands that are fighting the Anglo-Saxon invasion of the lands, those who reject occupation. This occupation is the real terrorism in this world.

As a result of the actions of this occupation, be it the killing of humans, the destruction of houses and trees, a group of free people in the world have moved to stand by the Iraqi and Palestinian peoples, as they continue to suffer from the evils of the occupation. Those volunteers include: Tom Fox, James Loney, Harmeet Sooden, and Norman Kember.

Those are the same friends of the martyr Rachel Corrie who was crushed under an Israeli bulldozer as she stood in the defense of our people and her friends against the Israeli Zionist occupation. We came to know them as they took a courageous stance against the new system of apartheid and the racist separation Wall. They suffered as we did, and were wounded by the bullets of the occupation, while others were exiled and imprisoned

Therefore, we ask the kidnappers to release those hostages in order for them to go back and stand by the side of justice and peace, and by the side of the persecuted nations, notwithstanding the actions of their governments who are directly responsible for all the violence in the region.

United together to eradicate the occupation and to lift the injustices from our peoples

Your brothers,

The Al Aqsa Martyrs Brigades

http://beirut.indymedia.org/ar/2005/12/3518.shtml

8. Sanded in Baghdad

Tom – Tuesday, July 12, 2005

Spending three days in the Baghdad airport waiting to see if the sand and dust would let up enough to allow flights to arrive (and then allow me to leave) was more stressful that I imagined. Of course, six trips on the airport road may have been a factor in increasing my stress level.

There were a number of internationals in the same predicament I was in. Many were people I've had very little contact with in my time in Iraq. Some were private security contractors who work for the large international firms like Dyncorp and KBR and are paid substantial sums (many 1,000 dollars a day) to protect international facilities and personnel. Others worked for NGO's and organizations that were business related, such as a firm that did management training for Iraqi entrepreneurs. I took the opportunity of being stuck there to try and get to know a number of them.

Perhaps the stress of cancelled flights and having to reschedule and arrange transport back to the Green Zone or other international facilities made their comments harsher than would be the case under different circumstances. But nonetheless, I was dismayed with what seemed, to me at least, to be very racist and colonialist statements by almost every contractor or entrepreneur I talked with.

Having grown up the Southern U.S. and having a very racist father, it was a very bizarre experience hearing almost the same comments being made against Iraqis that I heard as a child being made against blacks. The same venom, for lack of a better word, was coming out of their mouths as they denigrated the

31

people, culture and societal norms of Iraq.

Equally disturbing for me was the colonialist attitude of most of the business-connected internationals (most of the contractors I talked to were South African or English and most of the businessmen were American and all except one were white males). Remarks like, "We have to show them how it's really done", or "They don't have a clue how it's done in the West". There seemed, to me at least, to be no attempt at understanding, much less respecting, the culture of the people they ostensibly are here to work in partnership with.

I have to assume the racist attitudes of the security contractors stems from the necessity for a human being to dehumanize and marginalize another human being in order to kill them. Dehumanization is a mind game military leaders the world over have used to indoctrinate recruits with and it also seems to be the case with these mercenary soldiers.

The colonialist attitudes are harder to grasp. Is colonialism something unique to white, male Westerners? (And I include myself in this category.) Do we see Iraq the same way as Kipling saw India, that of being "the white man's burden" to bring Western civilization to the uncivilized Arabs and Kurds?

Those three days at the airport are woven deeply into my spirit. I'm wondering if I have swallowed poison that will harden or embitter me. Or perhaps I have been blessed with a homeopathic remedy of absorbing just enough poison to begin to cure me of my own subconscious racist and colonist tendencies and then be able to help others cure themselves. Time will tell.

Response by James L. Bevel

Tom Fox was out on the frontier in this day as were Chaney, Goodman and Schwerner in the Mississippi Summer Project (1964) and as were Jackson, Reeb, Liuzzo, and Daniels in the Alabama Right-to-Vote Movement (1965).

They all gave their lives to break through a shield of darkness that brought light and raised human consciousness to another level.

Forty years ago, the issue was, "Can wars be won without injury, threats, destruction of property, violence, or murder?"

The answer came rolling back, "Certainly, if there are those who are willing to put the nonviolent principle to the test." In that day, the mountain of segregation, discrimination and disenfranchisement loomed above the horizon of the human estate. It appeared to be insurmountable. But a few people took Jesus, Gandhi and Martin Luther King, Jr., for their word, moved on faith and tore the mountain down.

Today, we face the mountain of (1) murder (including abortion, capital punishment and war); (2) miseducation of children and citizens; (3) economic exploitation of animals and people; and (4) sexual perversity and brokenness in family life.

And we are all called to the frontier and battlefield by Tom Fox.

Let me quote Tom Fox: "To really create the peaceable realm on earth would require a tremendous deal of energy. Highly motivated and committed individuals and governments would need to expend a great deal of material resources to bring about peace."

In effect, that is a motion. Will we let the motion die for a lack of a second?

For this goal, like the early founders of our nation, we must give our lives, fortunes and sacred honor.

In nonviolence, when you have a problem, you must first identify it. Then you must decide whether to faint, fold, flee, or fight or you must hold fast to truth, stand firm on truth, maintain faith, and move forward on love. If the latter course of action is decided, then you must define the elements of the problem. In

33

defining the problem, you discover that you are contributing to the problem. This demands that you confess; the confession further demands that you repent. Take your investment out of the problem.

As you confess and repent, you also must begin to forgive and not judge others. This process is referred to as the due process of law. It carries you back to the cause of the problem.

Once the cause is discovered, you are able to formulate a plausible solution.

Then you begin to dialogue by (1) asking questions, (2) getting answers, (3) making decisions, and (4) doing work.

As you move forward, you will be attacked by hate, apathy, lust, and fear. You deal with each of these as you did the original problem (definition and due process) until you get to the cause and dissolve it.

You continue your ascendancy to the solution.

Tom Fox has a motion on the floor, and he is calling for the nonviolent army to join him in bringing authentic peace to the family of man.

For one, I would like to serve in the Tom Fox brigade.

Suggested Readings

The Sermon on the Mount by Jesus Christ

LeoTolstoy, *The Kingdom of God is Within You* by Leo Tolstoy

Mohandas K. Gandhi, *The Story of My Experiments With Truth*.

Joan Bondurant, *Conquest of Violence*.

Rev. James Luther Bevel was born in Itta Bena, Mississippi on October 19, 1936. He attended American Baptist College in Nashville, Tennessee. During this time, he studied Gandhi's nonviolent movement under the instruction of Jim Lawson in Nashville and later under Myles Horton at the Highlander Folk School, also in Tennessee. As a seminary student, Bevel helped to organize the Nashville Student Movement, which opened up lunch counters and theaters in the city of Nashville.

In 1960, Bevel was a co-founder of the Student Nonviolent Coordinating Committee (SNCC). Bevel appointed the ten Nashville students who continued the Freedom Rides in 1961, resulting in the desegregation of interstate travel. Between 1961-1963, Bevel organized the Mississippi Project and the Council of Federated Organizations (COFO).

In 1963, Dr. Martin Luther King, Jr., recognized Bevel as "an experienced leader" and asked him to direct the Southern Christian Leadership Conference's (SCLC) direct action campaign. Until the time of King's death in 1968, Bevel organized or directed all of the successful campaigns of the 1960s Civil Rights Movement, including the Birmingham Children's Crusade (1963), the March on Washington (1963), the Selma Right-to-Vote Movement (1965), the Chicago Open Housing Movement (1966), and the Mobilization to End the War in Vietnam (1967).

After King's death, Bevel developed the Nonviolent Clinical Process and the Precinct Council model of citizen self-governance. He has worked on behalf of many controversial leaders including Rev. Sun Myung Moon, economist Lyndon LaRouche, President Nelson Mandela, and the Honorable Minister Louis Farrakhan, who called Bevel the "Father of Atonement" for his contribution of the principle of atonement, which evolved into the historic Million Man March on October 16, 1995.

9. Alexander left Iraq and arrived safely

Tom – Thursday, 21 April 2005

   Alexander left Iraq and arrived safely in Amman, Jordan.

   The brother-in-law of detainee Mohammed Hashem Fathy al Allaf (part of CPT's Adopt-a-Detainee campaign) visited. He brought a friend, whose three-year-old son is paralyzed by cerebral palsy. Doctors have told the father that he should get treatment outside of Iraq. The father asked if CPT could help, so the team wrote a recommendation letter for him to take to an Iraqi doctor who arranges for treatment outside of the country.

   An Iraqi friend who is also a former detainee visited for supper (the friend's testimony will soon be located at http://www.cpt.org/iraq/iraqtestimonies.php). He, the MPT president, and the women's rights worker discussed the possibilities for MPT. All three insisted that they were not afraid of anyone who might be threatening the team.

Stanley Hauerwas

   A meaningless death – that's what the world must think about Tom Fox. A meaningless death. What a waste. A lovely, harmless, human being killed to know purpose. What a waste . . .

   Christian Peacemaker Teams–what a waste. They must be crazy! What in the world do they think they are doing. Showing up in Baghdad with no hope of making a difference against the power

36

of the United States military. Or better put, no hope of making a difference against the hubris of the United States presumption that everyone wants to be like us. Christian Peacemaker Teams is surely the craziest idea anyone could imagine. What a waste . . .

Such is the world's attitude toward deaths like Tom Fox's and the work of Christian Peacemaker Teams. Yet I believe without lives and deaths like Tom Fox we are without hope.

Yet I believe without lives like those exemplified my Christian Peacemaker Teams we are without hope. For lives like Tom Fox's life and work like Christiam Peacemaker Teams testify to the conviction that the only solution to big problems are small. Lives, small lives, like Tom Fox, are hope in a world gone mad. Lives like Tom Fox and the work of Christian Peacemaker Teams testify and witness to God's way with the world, that is, big problems only have small solutions.

The cross is God's small solution to the world's big problems. Peace simply names the time and action of making sure that a friend whose three-year-old son is paralyzed by cerebral palsy receives the care necessary to treat that illness. This is the kind of small solution that provides hope against the darkness of hate that has shaped American action in Iraq. Small acts of kindness amidst hate is the only hope we have.

Tom Fox was shaped by the silence of the Quaker meeting. A silence that witnesses to the small solution that was Christ, making possible a witness in the world that is the only appropriate response to the world's noisiness. It is the silence of Christ before Pilate that refuses to lie. It is the silence born of a patience that confronts the world's impatience making possible a life of nonviolence otherwise unavailable.

So of course the world thinks Tom Fox dies in vain. But we know he did not die in vain because he helped a three-year-old boy be cared for. His life makes possible our lives in which we too learn to continue the small acts of kindness necessary for there to be an alternative to a world gone mad due to its impatience. Thank God for a life like Tom Fox.

Stanley Hauerwas is Professor of Theological Ethics at Duke Divinity School, Durham North Carolina.

10. Uprooted –

Tom – Wednesday, January 05, 2005

    The Palestinian village of Jayyous is blessed. Blessed by a wonderful hilltop location looking over a fertile valley with olive trees, orange groves and greenhouses.

    The village of Jayyous is cursed. Cursed by the Israeli "security" fence that cuts the village off from the fields with one gate open three times a day to allow some (less than 10% of the villagers) to farm the land.

    The village of Jayyous may be doomed. The settlement of Zufin, which is entirely on the Palestinian side of the Green Line, is expanding. Not expanding towards Israel but expanding towards the olive groves of Jayyous.

    On December 31st [2004] over two hundred Israeli peace activists and dozens of internationals drove from Tel Aviv towards the fields of Jayyous to plant hundreds of saplings where part of the olive grove had been uprooted. Legal proceedings have put a temporary halt to the expansion but the settlers maintain that they have "bought" the land from an Israeli company. The activists were stopped by Israeli Defense Forces (IDF) and Israeli police some three miles outside the grove. They got out of their busses and walked the rest of the way with police and IDF taking pictures of them and shouting out on bullhorns, "This is private property belonging to the settlers".

    On the village side of the fence over a hundred Palestinian villagers and about twenty internationals (including two CPTers)

38

marched down the hill to find a way to come together with the Israelis who had planted the olive saplings. The march was organized by local civic and religious leaders and was totally nonviolent. The organizers had the kids carry the signs (it's harder to throw rocks with a sign in your hand) and kept everybody focused on standing firm against the IDF but not provoking them.

In between the two sides at the gate were an additional 60 IDF and about a dozen police. Intense negotiations ensued between the villagers and the IDF on one side and the Israeli activists and the IDF on the other side of the fence. Eventually four people (one Jayyous farmer and three Israelis) carried one of the uprooted trees that had been left to die through the gate to the village side to be replanted. One of Israelis who carried the tree said, "This is a token act of solidarity of the joint struggle of Israelis and Palestinians. It is a campaign that will continue to grow in strength until the walls and fences are brought down."

Uprooting an olive grove that has been fruitful for generations is a disheartening act. The sight of Palestinians and Israelis carrying a tree together to replant it is a hopeful act. The only thing that will tip the balance towards planting and away from uprooting is for all peoples, Jewish, Muslim and Christian to work together in solidarity. We must pray together. We must work together. We must continue to bring light to those from all faiths whose hearts are trapped in darkness. We must all find ways to root ourselves in the creation of peace.

Max Carter

A few years before his journey to Iraq, Tom developed an interest and expertise in British Quaker theologian Rex Ambler's Experiment with Light. The experiment recapitulates early Friends' process of centering down and accessing the power and vitality of the Light. Many of Tom's friends drew encouragement during his captivity knowing that he had confidence in the presence of that Light in all and could not only "answer it" but access it in himself and others.

39

So, how are we to understand the nature of people who could be in the presence of Tom and not only resist his attempts at appealing to that Light and power in them but, in the end, murder him in a vicious and callous way? It challenges the very core of Christian faith in love overcoming hate, good overcoming evil, and the Quaker testimony of the Light.

Wrestling with clear evidence that Tom was unable to "answer that of God" in his captors is hard, and Quaker lore ill equips us for such failure. Our typical stories are of Quakers "leaving the latchstring out" and having Indians pass by their frontier homes on raiding parties; of John Woolman's appealing successfully to slaveowners' sense of right; of Elizabeth Fry's moving unmolested among the "howling crowd" of prisoners in Newgate Gaol; of Rufus Jones convincing the Nazis to let Friends help Jews get out of Europe.

We are well advised to enter into work such as Tom's with a healthy respect for the possibility of failure. Quaker theology teaches that the inward Light can flicker, dim, and become hidden if resisted consistently. While people are not born good or bad, we make choices throughout our lives that place us under the influence of good or evil. I am perfectly comfortable in saying that Tom's captors were not under the influence of good when they killed him. Tom, however, was under the influence of good in offering his life as a living sacrifice for a truth that transcends his own life.

In that way, Tom, to paraphrase scripture, "saved his life even while losing it," for his life was "caught up in Christ," and the Christ spirit in which he lived could not be killed. In that sense, Tom's life and death is a light that continues to shine in the darkness, and the darkness cannot put it out. And we must also not give up the hope that perhaps, in some way, Tom was able to reach that of God in others – if not in his captors, then certainly in the many thousands around the world who were moved by his witness.

Contemplating Tom's death, I have been reminded of the story of Fr. Maximillian Kolbe, who volunteered to take the place of a prisoner condemned to the starvation bunker at Auschwitz. Reflecting on Kolbe's sacrifice, a fellow prisoner later wrote:

"We became aware someone among us in this spiritual dark night of the soul was raising the standard of love on high Therefore it is not true, we cried, that humanity is cast down and trampled in the mud, overcome by oppressors, and overwhelmed by hopelessness. Thousands of prisoners were convinced the true world continued to exist and that our torturers would not be able to destroy it. More than one individual began to look within himself for this real world, found it, and shared it with his camp companion, strengthening both in this encounter with evil His death was the salvation of thousands. And on this, I would say, rests the greatness of that death. That was a shock full of optimism, regenerating and giving strength; we were stunned by his act, which became for us a mighty explosion of light in the dark camp night ." *(A Man for Others*, 178)

We are, finally, accountable for living up to the Light we have, of doing what we know to be right, not determining our actions on the inability of others to live up to their best lights. It is a task not to be taken lightly.

Max Carter is Director of Friends Center and Quaker Studies and coordinator of campus ministries at Guilford College, Greensboro North Carolina.

Suggested Reading:

Rex Ambler, *Truth of the Heart: An Anthology of George Fox,* and

Light to Live By: An Exploration in Quaker Spirituality (Britain Yearly Meeting)

Peggy Gish, *Iraq: A Journey of Hope and Peace* (Herald Press)

11. Pressure Cooker

Tom – Wednesday, November 17, 2004

"People's homes are like the cells of a prison. And Iraq is the prison." A friend of CPT here in Baghdad gave this assessment of his country during a recent visit. His neighborhood is adjacent to an area that has been the scene of daily clashes between insurgents and Iraqi National Guard troops.

"Things are such in my country that we can't trust anybody. We don't know if we are with a friend or an enemy." Another friend used these words to describe how it feels to travel the roads outside of Baghdad.

Those of us here on the ground see a different picture of Iraq than the one being painted by the American government and some American media. It is also a different picture than the one being painted by some Arabic media and governments. It seems as if both Western and Middle Eastern governments and media are using broad brushstrokes to try and paint over each other's vision of events in this troubled land.

One analogy that seems relevant is that of a pressure cooker. For decades, the repressive regime of Saddam Hussein kept a lid on all the religious, ethnic and cultural tensions that exist in Iraq. Sunni and Shi'a have issues of trust that stretch back for centuries. Many of the Kurdish people of the north feel a need to create a separate country. There are tribal cultural issues that create tension within the country as well. Saddam and his henchmen repressed all of these tensions without doing anything to work on solutions. The lid of the pressure cooker was put on so tightly that when the Coalition forces blew the lid off in March of 2003 everything spewed all over the "kitchen". What seems to be happening right now is that the Interim Government of Iraq and the Multinational Forces are trying to scoop up the mess, throw it back into the pot and push another lid on it. They are recreating the same unresolved issues of conflict that have plagued the country for more than twenty years.

London, England, April 2006

Norman Kember – A Tribute to Tom Fox.

(Sent to a memorial meeting for Tom in Washington DC)

I write as one of the three people who spent many weeks with Tom before he was taken from us and killed.

Rather more reserved than the rest of us he forged a personal routine in captivity – from his 2 minute bath and regular exercise to our daily worship, Bible study and 30 minutes of silence which he valued. He was upset when other events interfered with these spiritual exercises.

He accepted that my experience of CPT was limited as I could not join in the extensive discussions he had with Jim of CPT successes and failures, of its policies and planning. His loyalty to the CPT ethic of nonviolence was outstanding.

He led worship in Quaker style and in Bible Study followed the four exercises for each, not always accurately, recalled passage: first impressions, relevance to our life experience, difficulties in understanding and how the message would change our life. His contributions to these discussions were often profound and based on his extensive reading. It was like having René Gerard present with us.

I remember Tom for his outstanding humanity. We often heard explosions in the city and he would pray for the victims and their families. He reminded us that our deprivations in captivity were paralleled by those in the lives of many in Iraq and the wider world. In captivity he volunteered to take on the greater discomforts.

In the many hours of talks together he gave us insights into his love of music, of the natural world and his family.

I salute Tom Fox.

– Norman Kember.

From Harmeet Sooden

His chained hand tucked me into bed most nights. I have no words of my own, no feelings:

When to the sessions of sweet silent thought
I summon up remembrance of things past,
I sigh the lack of many a thing I sought,
And with old woes new wail my dear time's waste:
Then can I drown an eye, unused to flow,
For precious friends hid in death's dateless night,
And weep afresh love's long since cancell'd woe,
And moan the expense of many a vanish'd sight:
Then can I grieve at grievances foregone,
And heavily from woe to woe tell o'er
The sad account of fore-bemoaned moan,
Which I new pay as if not paid before.
But if the while I think on thee, dear friend,
All losses are restored and sorrows end.

Sonnet XXX
William Shakespeare

12. The Middle of Nowhere

Tom – April 27, 2005

The ability to feel the pain of another human being is central to any kind of peace making work. But this compassion is fraught with peril. A person can experience a feeling of being overwhelmed. Or a feeling of rage and desire for revenge. Or a desire to move away from the pain. Or a sense of numbness that can deaden the ability to feel anything at all.

How do I stay with the pain and suffering and not be overwhelmed? How do I resist the welling up of rage towards the perpetrators of violence? How do I keep from disconnecting from or becoming numb to the pain?

After eight months with CPT, I am no clearer than I when I began. In fact I have to struggle harder and harder each day against my desire to move away or become numb. Simply staying with the pain of others doesn't seem to create any healing or transformation. Yet there seems to be no other first step into the realm of compassion than to not step away.

*"Becoming intimate with the queasy feeling of being in the middle of nowhere makes our hearts more tender. When we are brave enough to stay in the nowhere place then compassion arises spontaneously" (*The Places that Scare You *by Pema Chodron, page 120).*

Being in the middle of nowhere really does create a very queasy feeling and yet so many spiritual teachers say it is the only authentic place to be. Not staking out any ground for myself creates the possibility of standing with anyone. The middle of nowhere is the one place where compassion can be discovered. The constant challenge is recognizing that my true country of origin is the middle of nowhere.

In the Middle of Nowhere with Tom Fox and Pema Chodron

Sallie B. King

The April 27, 2005 entry shows Tom drawing from Buddhist teachers. It begins with Tom recounting his encounters with terrible human suffering. Tom reflects, "the ability to feel the pain of another human being is central to any kind of peace making work." Buddhist teachers often observe that the beginning of any kind of peace work is compassion, which means, specifically, caring about the suffering of others. Buddhist teacher Thich Nhat Hanh made this idea famous in his book, Being Peace, the main thesis of which was the idea that in order to make peace one must "be peace" first.

But how can one "be peace" if one follows another of Nhat Hanh's recommendations? When asked what we should do about the suffering of others, Nhat Hanh often says that there is no blueprint; the way to proceed is to stay with the suffering, and then something will occur to us to do. We want to turn away because seeing others suffering pains us we really are all empathetic by nature but we must stay with the suffering.

Yet as one who did exactly this, getting as close as he could to the pain of the Iraqi people, and staying with that pain, Tom reflected, "simply staying with the pain of others doesn't seem to create any healing or transformation. Yet there seems to be no other first step into the realm of compassion than to not step

46

away." He went on, "this compassion is fraught with peril. A person can experience a feeling of being overwhelmed. How do I stay with the pain and suffering and not be overwhelmed?" This, indeed, is a serious question, even for those of us who experience this pain muted through the media while in the safety and comfort of our homes. It treads on some of the deepest spiritual ground.

If staying with the pain is not enough, do we need something else? On 8/30/2005, Tom quoted Friend Elizabeth Blackwell, "I must have something in life which will fill this vacuum and prevent this sad wearing away of the heart." In the midst of the pain and madness of 4/27/2005 Tom quoted Pema Chodron, an American Buddhist teacher in the tradition of Tibetan Buddhism: "Becoming intimate with the queasy feeling of being in the middle of nowhere makes our hearts more tender. When we are brave enough to stay in the nowhere place then compassion arises spontaneously."

In a profound reflection on this quotation Tom wrote, "Being in the middle of nowhere really does create a very queasy feeling and yet so many spiritual teachers say it is the only authentic place to be. Not staking out any ground for myself creates the possibility of standing with anyone. The middle of nowhere is the one place where compassion can be discovered. The constant challenge is recognizing that my true country of origin is the middle of nowhere."

So, do we, as Pema Chodron and Tom Fox say, need to aim to be "in the middle of nowhere," which is "my true country of origin"? What is this "true country" which is "nowhere"? Are there two kinds, a positive which is our true country and a negative which makes us queasy? Can the negative open to the positive? Or, on the other hand, is what we need to "have something which will fill this vacuum?" These two possibilities sound opposite, but are these the same or are they different?

If we are headed for this "true country" of "nowhere," how do we get there? If we take the Meeting for Worship as a time of deep self-emptying, do we find our true country there?

47

After he had been entirely emptied by the blinding power of the Light, the apostle Paul said, "I live, not now I, but Christ in me." That's a Christian koan. Here's a Zen koan: "Show me your original face before your parents were born." Do these koans takes us to the same no-place? And how does all this relate to working in Iraq?

Sallie B. King is a member of Valley Friends Meeting in Harrisonburg, VA and a professor of philosophy and religion at James Madison University. She is a former co-Clerk of her monthly Meeting, a member of the Christian and Inter-faith Relations Committee of Friends General Conference, and a Trustee of the international, interfaith Peace Council. She is the author of *A Quaker Response to Christian Fundamentalism*, published by the Religious Education Committee of Baltimore Yearly Meeting, as well as several books on Buddhism and Buddhist-Christian dialogue.

For further reading:

Pema Chodron, *When Things Fall Apart: Heart Advice for Difficult Times* (Shambhala)

Thich Nhat Hanh, *Being Peace* (Parallax Press)

Robert Aitken and David Steindl-Rast, *The Ground We Share: Everyday Practice, Buddhist and Christian* (Shambhala)

13. Why? What? Who?

Tom – May 17, 2005

    The 17th century English philosopher Thomas Hobbes described the ultimate nightmare of any society as being "the war of the all against the all." Such is the state of existence here in Iraq. When the U.S. led invasion tore away the facade of the state of Iraq a torrent of religious, ethnic, tribal and cultural tensions that had festered for generations was unleashed. I have not heard one person say that Saddam was a wise or revered leader. But I have heard many people say that while they lived under the threat of violence with Saddam, they prefer that life to the bloodshed, chaos and anarchy that surrounds them now.

    No one seems to offer a solution that does not entail more guns, more restrictions on basic human rights, more soldiers, more barbed wire and concrete barricades, more "security" and less freedom. Sooner or later the insurgency will run out of suicide bombers and weapons. Sooner or later the ringleaders will be captured or killed. But what will remain will be one of most restrictive, oppressive police states in the world.

    "Spreading freedom and democracy." "The war of the all against the all." It was a fairly quiet day in Baghdad.

Reflection by Rubye Howard Braye

John 10:17 "Therefore My Father loves Me, because I lay down My life that I may take it again. No one takes it from Me, but I lay it down of Myself. I have power to lay it down, and I have power to take it again. This command I have received from My Father."

The military sends soldiers around the world into all types of armed conflicts to alter the course of events. Many return. Some do not.

Representatives of nongovernmental organizations frequently go to many of the same places to serve. They have similar expectations and outcomes.

Upon hearing that Tom Fox had joined Christian Peacemaker Teams and was headed to Iraq, it was clear that he had a heart to serve and longed to make a difference nonviolently. The outcome at no time seemed to be in his favor. Knowing this, he left behind many who prayerfully supported him. For months, he posted thoughtful blog entries that explained what he saw and heard. Based on what he wrote, he was not a bystander and knew that it was possible that he would be called to make what soldiers call "the supreme sacrifice."

He got the call. When the violent end came, his attackers probably thought that they had won; but, that is not true. He volunteered to go to Iraq. He loved God and loved the people of Iraq. He gave his life.

Before he was killed, he wrote with clarity and conviction of the horrors that he witnessed. He asked many questions that he could not answer. Most remain unanswered. In May 2005, Tom wrote the message cited above. As I write a year later, the situation is such that the same queries could be written: *Why? What? Who?*

If we had the courage to ask, the answers to some of these questions would say a lot about who we are as Christians. What will it take for us to live lives of peace? Are the lives that we live based on love? What are we willing to give to promote peace locally, nationally, and around the world? While the answers are just words, it seems appropriate to share some of Tom's last words written on November 8, 2005.

What words or deeds could undo the massive trauma faced by the people of Fallujah every day? Everywhere we went during the afternoon young boys listened to our words and the words of those with whom we were meeting. I kept wondering what was going on in their minds as they relived the events of a year ago and the ensuing trauma. What effect will these events have on their lives as they grow up?

There are no words.

There may not be words, but the life that Tom gave spoke and continues to speak. May our lives speak, too?

References

The Gospel of John

Hobbes, T. (1991). *Man and Citizen*. Indianapolis, IN: Hackett Publishing Company.

Rubye Howard Braye lives in Wilmington, NC, where she worships as a member of the Wilmington Friends Meeting, NCYM(C).

14. "A Statement of Conviction"

Annie Dillard – "Every live thing is a survivor on a kind of extended emergency bivouac. But at the same time we are also created. In the Koran, Allah asks, "The heaven and the earth and all in between, thinkest thou I made them in jest?"

"There is not a guarantee in the world. Oh your needs are guaranteed, your needs are absolutely guaranteed by the most stringent of warranties, in the plainest, truest words: knock, seek, ask. But you must read the fine print. 'Not as the world giveth, give I unto you.' That's the catch . . . . You see the needs of your own spirit met whenever you have asked, and you have learned that the outrageous guarantee holds. You see the creatures die, and you know you will die. And one day it occurs to you that you must not need life. Obviously.

"Divinity is not playful. The universe was not made in jest but in solemn incomprehensible earnest There is nothing to be done about it, but ignore it, or see. And then you walk fearlessly – like the monk on the road who knows precisely how vulnerable he is, who takes no comfort among death-forgetting men, and who carries his vision of vastness and might around in his tunic like a live coal which neither burns nor warms him, but with which he will not part."

– Pilgrim at Tinker Creek

In October of 2004, the Christian Peacemaker team in Baghdad was down to two people. With the city awash in violence, CPT had not replaced departed volunteers. CPT's work in Iraq was at a standstill as staff tried to discern how, or even whether, it could operate without taking foolish risks.

Matt Chandler, a recent college graduate, was one of those two hardy CPT peacemakers, the "Team Coordinator" for Baghdad that fall. Tom Fox was all that was left of the team he coordinated.

On October 19, Margaret Hassan was kidnapped. Once this prominent Iraqi humanitarian worker was taken hostage, it was absolutely clear that no one was safe.

On October 20, Tom and Matt composed a "Statement of Conviction":

"We, members of Christian Peacemaker Teams (CPT) in Iraq, are aware of the many risks both Iraqis and internationals currently face. However, we are convinced at this time that the risks, while significant, do not outweigh our purpose in remaining

As a peacemaking team we need to cross boundaries to help preserve what is human in all of us and so offer glimpses of hope in a dark time.

We reject kidnapping and hostage-taking wholesale. If any of us are taken hostage, absolutely no ransom will be paid. In such an event, CPT will attempt to communicate with the hostage-takers or their sponsors and work against journalists' inclination to vilify and demonize the offenders. We will try to understand the motives for these actions, and to articulate them, while maintaining a firm stance that such actions are wrong

We reject the use of violent force to save our lives We forgive those who consider us their enemies. Therefore, any penalty should be in the spirit of restorative justice, rather than in the form of violent retribution.

We hope that in loving both friends and enemies and

53

by intervening non-violently to aid those who are systematically oppressed, we can contribute in some small way to transforming this volatile situation."

God's fallen world is both beautiful and terrible. Both joy and suffering inundate us. Tom knew this, and knew how vulnerable he was.

Tom may be the first to die of hostile action while serving in a Christian nonviolent intervention. He will not be the last. But as long as sacrificial Christian peacemaking persists, Tom Fox will be remembered for carrying with him a vision of vastness and might with which he would not part. And neither should we.

Ron Mock is associate professor of political science and peace studies at George Fox University in Newberg, Oregon, where he lives with his wife and two of his four children. He got his start in peace studies when he diverted from a budding legal career to help start a Christian mediation service in the Detroit, Michigan area. Since then he has studied peacemaking at a range of levels, from interpersonal to international.

His latest works are *When the Rain Returns: Toward Justice and Reconciliation in Palestine and Israel,* (American Friends Service Committee, 2004), which he co-wrote with the other members of the International Quaker Working Party on Middle East Peace; and *Loving Without Giving In: Christian Responses to Terrorism and Tyranny* (Cascadia Press, 2004), which is all his own fault.

15. "Each of You Must Be Quick to Listen–"

Tom – From a talk given at Northern Virginia Mennonite Church on Feb. 27th, 2005:

Being part of Christian Peacemaker Teams in Iraq has led me to many "firsts"– first time in the Middle East, first time in a war zone, first time being targeted as "the enemy" due to being an American. Now the first time to stand before a religious community as a member of CPT and give a talk during a worship service. And I would have to say that I am more nervous about this "first" than I was about the others.

As a member of a silent Quaker Meeting one aspect of the Mennonite tradition I have learned to appreciate is that of looking to Scripture as a basis for one's spiritual journey . . . . This is from the first chapter of James, verses 19-22. "Each of you must be quick to listen, slow to speak and slow to be angry. For a person's anger cannot promote the justice of God. Away then with all that is unclean, and the malice that hurries to excess. Quietly accept the messages planted in your hearts, which can bring you salvation. Only be sure that your act on the messages and do not merely listen to them."

We did a lot of listening in Iraq with CPT and the stories we heard were not always easy to hear. And after hearing them I would often find myself becoming quick to pass judgment on others and quick to become angry.

The first times I participated in human rights documentation was last September. We interviewed an Iraqi,

Dr. Ammad, who had been detained by American forces in May of 2003. He was imprisoned for six months during which time he was subjected to many of the interrogation methods you are all too familiar with . . . .

But in any case I was taking the notes as he described how they pulled out one of his fingernails. I listened as he described the beatings and showed us the scars. I felt myself becoming very angry at the thought of these horrible actions being done by my own countrymen and women . . . .

One thing that has been in my heart the most in these first months of being a part of CPT has been getting to know people (both within CPT and with other peace and violence reduction organizations) who have committed themselves to not giving in to anger when faced with injustice. But, and perhaps I am wrong, I have also experienced the sense that a number of these people have been affected by being exposed to so much violence and anger and retaliatory violence.

Many I have experienced as being bitter – as if they have encased themselves in a hard shell to protect their hearts from exposure to the pain and suffering they live with daily. Others I have experienced as being burdened – as if they have absorbed much pain and suffering to try and lighten the load for those they live with daily.

Must these be the alternatives to a violent response to anger?

James says that, "A person's anger cannot promote the justice of God." No matter if we succumb to anger, harden ourselves against anger or absorb anger; none of these ways can promote the justice of God. But does that mean we are not allowed to feel anger?

James says that we need to be slow to anger and that first we need to listen carefully, next to put some words to our feelings and then finally express our anger. But clearly he does not say "never become angry". However he does say that our response to anger, no matter what form it takes, cannot promote God's justice. So then what do we do with our anger? James says we need to turn that anger over to God and then, "Quietly accept the messages planted in our hearts".

Ched Myers

Two Martyrs Reflect on Anger and Justice

Jan Luiken (1649 - 1712) The Martyrdom of James, in *The Martyrs Mirror*.

"Know this, beloved brothers and sisters. Let each of you be quick to hear, slow to speak, and slow to anger. For our anger does not achieve the justice of God. Therefore put away all disrespectful behavior and overflowing malice, and receive with gentleness the implanted word, which is able to save your souls. But be doers of the word, and not hearers only, deceiving yourselves." (James 1:19-22)

The apostle James was the leader of the Jerusalem church in the second generation of the Jesus movement. According to tradition he was the brother of Jesus (imagine his childhood!). And this epistle exhibits the spirit and voice of the Jesus we encounter in the synoptic gospels. It also echoes the great 8th century prophets of Israel, particularly concerning the unacceptability of economic stratification among the people of God (see Jas 2:6f and 5:3-6).

James' sober class analysis evades our contemporary churches, and his "edge" led Luther and others to try to excise this epistle from the New Testament canon. He faced similar opposition in his own time: the ancient Jewish historian Josephus wrote that James was martyred in 63 C.E. during a security sweep that targeted those who were perceived by the Roman rulers of Palestine to be subversive to imperial order.

So it is significant that Tom Fox chose this epistle for a 2005 sermon (the first he had ever given!) at Northern Virginia Mennonite Church, a year and a half before his own martyrdom. But Fox chose as his focus not James' fiery exhortations to social justice, but rather the epistle's other main theme: his plea to believers to "walk the talk" (1:23-27) and to "tame the tongue" (3:1-12).

It is not surprising that Fox, by all accounts a quiet and humble advocate, would be attracted to James' dialectical call to unequivocal yet self-critical advocacy. After all, his Quaker tradition values an economy of words on one hand, and the creative power of "seeing what Love can do" on the other. (A famous story relates how unassuming Friends serving to reconstruct post-World War II Europe were once told that they ought to "preach what they practice.")

Our text invites disciples to confront their own anger, something Tom rightly identifies as a struggle for activists who immerse themselves in situations of discrimination, marginalization and violence. The word in Greek is *orgee,* a noun which occurs in the New Testament 36 times, mostly in reference to the "wrath" of God that human depravity elicits. The few times the word refers to human anger are warnings to believers (Eph 4:31; I Tim 2:8), most significantly in Romans 12:19: "Beloved, never avenge yourselves, but leave it to the *orgee* of God; for it is written, 'Vengeance is mine, I will repay, says the Lord'."

What the "wrath" of a nonviolent God might mean is surely a mystery; but it was clear to James that human exercise of *orgee* "cannot accomplish (Greek *katergazomai*) the justice of God" (1:20). Tom intuited deeply the truth of this difficult teaching, as his sermon attests. He embraced the apostle's reminder that only the "testing of our faith can accomplish (Gk *katergazomai*) patience" (1:3) in his call for activists to "work through their anger and come out the other side committed to peace."

I did not know Tom Fox, but every testimony I have encountered by or about him suggests that he walked this talk as few North American peacemakers have. And like James, Tom paid the ultimate price for nonviolently resisting an imperial war. The life and death of the Quaker peacemaker faithfully illuminates that of the apostle. And both invite us to deeper discipleship.

Ched Myers is an activist theologian, writer and popular educator who has worked for three decades with faith-based peace and justice concerns. He currently serves with Bartimaeus Cooperative Ministries in southern California (www.bcm-net.org).

Recommended reading: Elsa Tamez, *The Scandalous Message of James* (NY:Crossroad, 1990).

16. *Faces of Desperation*

Tom – Friday, October 21, 2005

     We are gathered around a campfire sharing chai (tea) and fellowship. "We" consists of nineteen Palestinian men women and children (ages one to thirteen) who have either been born in or have lived most of their lives in Iraq. "We" also consists of three CPTers, one member of the Muslim Peacemaker Teams and CPT's translator (who is also Palestinian). We are camped at the Al Walid border crossing between Syria and Iraq and are awaiting news from the Syrian government. News of whether or not the Iraqi Palestinians, who are currently barred from entering Syria, will be granted refugee status by the United Nations, which will be recognized by the Syrian government.

     But why would these people want to leave Iraq now? Iraq is now on its way to democracy. The tyrannical regime of Saddam Hussein has been gone for two and one half years. The reason is quite simple; the new Iraq government's security forces have made Iraqi Palestinians primary targets for harassment, arbitrary arrest, torture-induced confessions to crimes they didn't commit and in some cases death. All in the name of demonstrating how well the government's campaign of ridding Iraq of foreign terrorists is going.

     But why the Iraqi Palestinians? First they are easy to find. Most live in two large compounds in Baghdad. Second, they are defenseless. Iraqi Palestinians are barred from owing firearms. Third, they have no political clout. They can't vote, own property or even own a car. Fourth, they are small in numbers. The total population in Iraq is around 23,000. Fifth, Saddam used them to promote his political prestige with Sunni Arabs in the Middle East by giving them subsidized housing, a fact that was resented by many Iraqis. They were forced out of those apartments during the first months of the U.S. led invasion.

So here we are gathered around a campfire in the desert. We spent the first night sleeping on the sidewalk at the Syrian side of the border crossing. Trucks roared by all night making sleep almost impossible. Yet several said it was the best nights sleep they had gotten in months. No sirens, no gunfire, no house raids in the middle of the night, no one being hauled away by Iraqi security forces perhaps never to be seen again.

[From Monday, October 10th - The five children (ages 1 to 13) are getting bored and anxious. CPTer Sheila Provencher and the CPT translator have decided to start a one-hour "school" every morning for the older children. Provencher will teach English and the translator will do art. The first English lesson is teaching words about the weather using the "Itsy, Bitsy Spider" song.*]*

October 21, continued: Now into our eighth day we are living in tents provided by the UN. We are eating two meals a day in the border-crossing cafeteria thanks to the UN as well. . . . As I am writing this the men are playing a game of soccer and we wait. Wait to see if the UN and Syria can reach a solution to this humanitarian crisis.

I asked one man what he would do if the UN and Syria were unable to reach a solution and they were told to return to Iraq. Would he, and his family, return? "Never," he said, "We will either stay here or die before we return to the certain death of Iraq." I cannot imagine the level of desperation a person must reach in order to make such a statement. And yet, I don't need to imagine it at all. I see it on the faces of the community we are part of every day

---

Sheila Provencher

Dear Tom,

I wish that everyone I love could have met you too. I keep crying but I also feel overwhelmed by the gift of having known you and loved you, my beloved uncle – "Amu Tom" as all the Iraqi and

61

Palestinian children called you. How could we have had such a gift in you? You were gentleness, patience, compassion, forgiveness, and courage.

I cannot believe how patient you always were with me. When I walked into the kitchen in CPT's apartment in Baghdad and flipped out because the person ahead of me on the job chart had not prepared the water for the day, you just smiled and listened and excused all my crabbiness as the result of stress. You were always one of the people I could confide in.

Every morning in "no man's land" between Iraq and Syria with the Palestinian refugees, we got up and sat outside our tent, and you read from "The Cloud of Unknowing" and I read from the Liturgy of the Hours. Then we would talk about what message we each "got" at the time. It was my favorite half-hour of the day.

When the Red Sox finally won the World Series after 86 years, and my parents were so excited to share the news with me that they phoned Baghdad and accidentally woke you up at 6:00am Baghdad time, and you answered the phone but I was still in Amman and had not yet arrived, and in fact you and I had not even met yet, and here you were listening to these crazy people screaming about how the Red Sox had finally won, you just smiled and said "Well, I'm happy for you," even though you did not even know what was going on. When I met you the next day you told me that my parents had called.

You cooked like a master while claiming it was simple. "Anything tastes good if you add enough butter to it." I still wonder if you ever cooked for the people who took you. If they let you, I am sure that you would have.

The night before I left Baghdad in November 2005, two nights before you were taken, you led the good-bye prayer service. You said to me, "I don't know why, I just have this feeling that I want to do a Eucharist service for you. Don't ask me why a Quaker would lead a Eucharist, but I have a feeling this is what we're supposed to do." So we broke bread and drank grape juice and all shared the communion prayer, men and women taking turns. I think Anita wound up with the actual words of consecration. Afterwards you joked about this being your First Communion, at age 54, and we took pictures of me giving you communion, you kneeling like a devout altar boy. Laughing in the candlelight.

Six mornings a week, this past Fall, you would do yoga on the roof, greeting the sun as it peeked over the Baghdad skyline. I was on the other side of the roof, jumping rope and walking in circles around the whole roof, passing you in your meditation. I can still see you in my mind, stretching out like a tree with the dawn on your face.

I can hear your voice in my heart. You say things like, "Well, this was what was supposed to happen." "I'm just glad I could be here to help." "You keep taking care of yourself, now." Your one deep pain was knowing the anguish that your suffering could cause your children. You loved them so much, always sharing pictures and stories of them with all of our Iraqi and Palestinian friends.

We met in October 2004, right after Margaret Hassan had been killed. You, Matthew, and I were the whole team in Baghdad, and we talked about kidnapping, what could happen to us, and if we should stay in Iraq. You wrote a statement of conviction that included the words, "If I am ever called upon to make the ultimate sacrifice in love of enemy, I trust that God will give me the grace to do so." You did it, Tom. You were faithful until the very end. I imagine that even when you were about to die, you looked with forgiveness at the man who would kill you.

You bore in your own body the sufferings of everyone who has also been tortured and killed.

God, help us to be as faithful.

Sheila Provencher was Tom Fox's CPT teammate in Baghdad.

17. Two entries about young Friends, on a Tennessee blog, responding to an article about Tom's kidnaping.

Re: Tom Fox, Peace Activist and Former Chattanoogan, Remains Hostage in Iraq by nnnnn

07 Dec 2005 *Tom Fox was my first day school (sunday school) teacher, and I am lucky that I am able to say that. He devoted his life to helping people, no matter what the cost. I think Tom Fox is one of the bravest men I will have ever known. You may say he's stupid and naive, but he was living his life out for a higher purpose. I don't understand what gives you the right to judge the man. It doesn't matter what his captors thought. That's not why he was there. He was there to help, no matter what.All I can do is pray for you, and pray for peace.*

Re: Tom Fox, Peace Activist and Former Chattanoogan, Remains Hostage in Iraq by hhhhh

11 Dec 2005 *Thank you . . .for this article. I worked for a week with Tom this summer (in the kitchen at a Quaker camp) while he was between trips to Iraq. He led a workshop in which my daughter participated. He told of how once, while surrounded by soldiers in Iraq, he prayed for them, he sent powerful prayers for them—not for his release. They dispersed. Free from committing an act of violence upon an innocent person, and thereby releasing him as well. I guess this is what Jesus meant when he said, "Love your enemies."*

[Note: names have been removed.]

Reflection by Mali Royer

When I was a member of the Baltimore Yearly Meeting Young Friends Executive Committee, things fell into this pattern: we'd all be hanging out, the conferences were going great, and then some concerned adult would write a letter: Young Friends were making too much of a mess or we were smoking too much or our newsletter was too vulgar or we were kissing too much or whatever.

So the Executive Committee would meet, and at first we would be outraged and self-righteous. How dare they think that about us?

Tom Fox was a Friendly Adult Presence (FAP), so he sat in on the Executive Committee meetings. Each time we had to deal with such a letter, Tom said the same thing, "This is your community, and it is your responsibility to make things right."

So, after a little more grumbling, we would get to work, which usually meant a 60 person 2AM business meeting. We wouldn't just try to brush the concern under the rug, we really dissected the issues and make some lasting solutions so that at the next conference we wouldn't have to do this again.

When our discussions got really difficult and really intense, sometimes we would look to Tom, hoping he would give us a hint. But Tom would be asleep, his bald head tilted over the back of the bench and that serene smile on his face. I don't think he was smiling because he knew the answer, I think he was smiling because he knew we would find the answer.

Sometimes it was really hard, and sometimes it took a really long time, but we always did find some solution eventually. It was empowering to feel that we had taken responsibility for our community, and we were brought closer together in the knowledge that we all felt our community was worth working for.

Looking at the way Tom Fox lived his life, it is clear to me now that he didn't just mean, "this community Young Friends is your responsibility," he meant, "this community The World is your responsibility." Tom looked around this world and saw a lot of things going wrong, and decided to do something to try to fix things.

A lot of people who have criticized the Christian Peacemaker Teams say it is absurd to think you can send four people to Iraq and stop the war. And it is. But that isn't what they were trying to do.

When I was fifteen, I was food planner for the Thanksgiving conference at Homewood Friends Meeting. The first night of the conference, I was in the kitchen, trying to cook soup and nachos for 70 teenagers by myself.

Tom came into the kitchen just as I had managed to make a can of condensed tomato soup explode all over myself and the kitchen.

He said, "whatcha doing?," and I said I was cooking dinner, and he said, "You don't have to do that by yourself, you know." He disappeared from the kitchen and reappeared with seven young Friends who had volunteered to help me. From then on, whenever I saw someone cooking or cleaning or washing dishes at a conference, I joined them.

When I remember Tom Fox, when I miss him, I try to remember these two lessons. The community is our responsibility, but we don't have to do it all on our own. Tom didn't expect to stop the war and save the world all by himself. He just happened to step up first. And if we value this world and I think it's the best one we've got we have to admit it is worth the work and the sacrifice that it's going to take to fix things.

Mali Royer is a member of Homewood Friends Meeting in Baltimore, Maryland. She graduated from the Friends School of Baltimore in 2002 and attended Young Friends conferences throughout highschool. Mali graduated from Washington College in May 2006 with majors in Biology and Drama. She currently works as a nanny and plans to begin medical school in 2007.

18. Promoting the Justice of God

Tom – Feb. 27th, 2005

After I left Iraq in December (2004) I spent several weeks with the CPT project team in Hebron in the West Bank. Another CPTer and I traveled to the Palestinian village of Jayyous (which is near Ramallah) to participate in an action related to the Israeli security fence . . . .

One of the most positive experiences I had during my time in the Middle East happened in that same village . . . .

The villagers have plenty to be angry about. The village is separated from its fields, olive groves and greenhouses by the security fence. There is a gate that is opened three times daily to let some (less than 10% of the villagers have permits) to go across and work their crops. Even more of a threat is that an Israeli colony (the Arabic word for settlement is also the Arabic word for colony) is expanding towards their olive groves.

But rather than resort to violence or denial or shame as a response to their justifiable anger the village council worked through their anger and came out on the other side- the side of peaceful non-violent direct actions. In the action that I joined that Friday in January over two hundred citizens of Israel (mostly from the Gush Shalom peace organization) along with some Jayyous farmers and about fifty internationals spent the morning planting olive tree saplings in the area that had been bulldozed as part of the expansion plan. The destruction had been halted, at least for the present, by an Israeli court order (the colony is over ten kilometers on the Palestinian side of the Green Line, the UN recognized boundary between Israel and the West Bank).

After the planting they peacefully marched towards the security fence. At the same time after Friday prayers most of the

67

village (about one hundred and fifty) along with about twenty internationals peacefully marched down the hill to their side of the security fence. During the weeks of planning the Israeli and Palestinian activists came up with the idea to negotiate a symbolic "crossing" of the security fence with an olive tree from the uprooted grove to be replanted in the village.

It took an hour of hard negotiating with the hundred or so heavily armed Israeli troops but in the end three Israelis and one Palestinian took an olive tree across the barrier and gave it to the owner of the grove that had been uprooted (he did not at that time have a permit to cross the fence to work his lands).

It was a tiny thing – but it was totally peaceful and there was a sense of joy and celebration and much waving of hands in a spirit of friendship and peace between the Palestinians on one side and the Israelis on the other. And the press coverage of the event (both Palestinian and Israeli) was uniformly positive.

Skip Schiel

The ability to feel the pain of another human being is central to any kind of peace making work. But this compassion is fraught with peril. A person can experience a feeling of being overwhelmed. Or a feeling of rage and desire for revenge. Or a desire to move away from the pain. Or a sense of numbness that can deaden the ability to feel anything at all.

Tom Fox was in Hebron with the Christian Peacemaker Team for a short period in early 2005. In holy Hebron, where Abraham and family are buried, honored by the Ibrahimi mosque and synagogue complex, sacred to Jews, Christians, and Muslims, there is much to be angry about. I was there around the same time and may have met Tom.

CPT has two bases in Palestine in the Old City, not far from the tombs, established in 1995 after a massacre in the Ibrahimi mosque by an extreme orthodox Jew, Baruch Goldstein from Brooklyn, and in the Southern Hebron Hills, in the village of At-Tuwani.

In 2004, at the invitation of the people of At-Tuwani, CPT established its second base. One of their missions was to escort children to and from school past an Israeli settlement or colony. On one of these occasions, not far from the poisoning site I visited in March 2006, settlers wearing black face masks and talking in American accented English attacked two CPTers, Kim Laherty and Chris Brown, who were accompanying children past one of the settlements near At-Tuwani. They stole mobile phones and wallets, punctured a lung, and broke a leg, but the children were safe. Kim believes that partly as a result of this incident and CPT's continuing presence in At-Tuwani, the Israeli civil authority finally gave the villagers a permit to build a medical clinic, an unprecedented act, and only possible, Kim believes, because of the international presence and consequent international attention

In March 2006, I was with CPT again as they investigated a case of Israeli settlers poisoning the water and land of a shepherd family near At-Tuwani. We gathered testimony. Unfortunately that's about all CPT and the other 2 or 3 organizations that have talked with the shepherds whose goats were killed could do. It must be frustrating: someone poisons your goats, your main livelihood, on your own land, where your people have lived for centuries. The poisoners are newcomers, claiming their god gave them this land. Says so in the Bible. Here, look – a covenant. Thus: proved, get off this land or you die, slowly or quickly.

Besides escorting school children, helping a file lawsuits, vigiling at a police stations, CPT will also try to stop a soldier from detaining a young Palestinian man or stand between ravaging young settler girls spitting and cursing at young Palestinian school children.

One word for me sums up the situation in the territories: impunity. Israel does what it wishes, argues as it likes or presents no argument, and tightens the matrix of control. While the US, in the form most obviously of the administration and Congress, but also the general population, not only agrees but funds this criminal policy. International law, affirmed by many UN resolutions, forbids confiscation of land during an occupation.

The law is clear, the morality is clear, but without vigilant implementation, people suffer unjustly. The shepherd family lives a nightmare. And who cares? Good reason to be angry. Hard to be compassionate. What to do?

One answer is witness, taking a risk observing, reporting, inserting one's body in the machinery of oppression as Tom and his colleagues were doing in Iraq when kidnapped. The cost of such witness may be high, but as Dr. Martin Luther King Jr was fond of saying the arc of the universe is long but it bends toward justice.

> . . . *Resistance as spectacle has cut loose from its origins in genuine civil disobedience and is becoming more symbolic than real. Colorful demonstrations and weekend marches are fun and vital, but alone they are not powerful enough to stop wars. Wars will be stopped only when soldiers refuse to fight, when workers refuse to load weapons onto ships and aircraft, when people boycott the economic outposts of Empire that are strung across the globe.*

> *— Arundhati Roy*

Photos: link to my Southern Hebron Hills photos and story, March 15, 2006:

http://teeksaphoto.org/Levant2006/Images/Web_03_14_06_HebronHills/index.html

Skip Schiel is a Quaker photographer based in Cambridge, Massachusetts. Photographing a variety of themes such as poverty, water, American Indians, South Africa, and a racially mixed Quaker church in Chicago, I am now working on an extended project about the conditions and struggles in the so-called Holy Land. Working with the light known as Mediterranean and the light from the wisdom teachers found on this holy ground, I hope to open eyes and hearts of those in a nation that is one of the most responsible agents for the continuing suffering in Palestine and Israel.

Recommended books:

The Question of Palestine, Edward Said

When the Rains Return: Toward Peace and Reconciliation in Palestine and Israel, prepared by an International Quaker Working

Party on Israel and Palestine, AFSC, 2004.

How Long, O Lord? Christian, Jewish, and Muslim Voices From the Ground and Visions for the Future in Israel/Palestine, edited by Robert and Maurine Tobin.

Photos & writing (including new work from Palestine & Israel, Testing the Waters):

http://teeksaphoto.org

To join my email list for reports from this journey:

skipschiel@gmail.com with SUBSCRIBE in the heading

19. There Are No Words

Tom – Tuesday, November 08, 2005

"The ongoing difficulties faced by Fallujans are so great that words fail to properly express it." Words from a cleric in Fallujah as he tried to explain the litany of ills that continue to afflict his city one year after the U.S.-led assault took place.

"All the men in the mosque were from my neighborhood. They were not terrorists." Words from a young man who said he left a room of men either injured or homeless thirty minutes before the raid on his mosque, the same mosque shown in the now-famous videotape of an American soldier shooting unarmed men lying on the mosque floor.

"There haven't been any funds for home reconstruction available since the change in Iraqi government last January." The words of a civic leader from Fallujah as he showed CPTers the still-devastated areas of his city.

There are no words. A city that has been demonized by Americans and many Iraqis, using the words "the city of terrorists." A city that its residents call "the city of mosques." A city that even its residents have to enter at checkpoints, often taking up to an hour to traverse. A city that is being choked to death economically by those same checkpoints.

CPTers and a member of the Muslim Peacemaker Teams came to Fallujah to meet with friends and contacts to ask them if the city was planning on doing something in remembrance of the tragic events of last November when U.S. forces attacked their city of 300,000 to root out, by U.S. estimates, 1,500 terrorists.

What we heard in response were words of remembrance, resistance and resilience. The cleric said that a number of civic

72

leaders had come to him with a proposal for an action in remembrance of the anniversary. Their proposal was to raise funds to contribute to relief efforts for the victims of the earthquake in Pakistan. He said that a teaching of Islam is to always look to aid others in need before asking for aid yourself.

The cleric said that he recently traveled to another Middle Eastern country and during his visit he met with a cleric from Libya. The Libyan cleric said that in his city, and in other places in Libya, parents are naming newborn girls "Fallujah" in honor of the city. The cleric said that more than 800 girls had been named Fallujah in his city alone.

Words are inadequate, but words are all we have. Words like "collective punishment" and "ghettoize" come to mind for the current state of life in Fallujah.

What words or deeds could undo the massive trauma faced by the people of Fallujah every day? Everywhere we went during the afternoon young boys listened to our words and the words of those with whom we were meeting. I kept wondering what was going on in their minds as they relived the events of a year ago and the ensuing trauma. What effect will these events have on their lives as they grow up?

There are no words

Generosity and Bravery: What shall we give?

Lisa Schirch

The hugs were long and wet as I parted from my husband, daughter, and son in the parking lot at Dulles airport to board a plane to Lebanon and then Iraq to work with Mennonite Central Committee in August 2005. My friends chided me for going to a war zone while my children are so young. I felt united with the men and women in uniform who also stood at airports on that day, departing from their families, despite our very different plans for engaging with Iraqis.

I imagine Tom Fox's children hugged him in much the

same way that mine did when he left for Iraq. And I learned in Iraq that the Iraqis I was working with left their families in just as tearful a way every morning as they set off to build bridges across the lines of conflict in Iraq by building wells, starting health education, and micro-credit loan projects.

The tears were no choice for them; their own children's future is at stake. How do we each decide how much to sacrifice of our own lives to save the lives of others or to promote some principle we hold dear?

Tom writes that when he sat with Muslim clerics in Fallujah to hear of the devastation there, they instead talked about their concern for the people in Pakistan after the devastating earthquake. *"Their proposal was to raise funds to contribute to relief efforts for the victims of the earthquake in Pakistan. The Cleric said that a teaching of Islam is to always look to aid others in need before asking for aid yourself."*

It is hard to imagine that level of generosity. Mark 12: 41-44 reads "Jesus sat down opposite the place where the offerings were put and watched the crowd putting their money into the temple treasury. Many rich people threw in large amounts. But a poor widow came and put in two very small copper coins, worth only a fraction of a penny. Calling his disciples to him, Jesus said, "I tell you the truth, this poor widow has put more into the treasury than all the others. They all gave out of their wealth; but she, out of her poverty, put in everything all she had to live on."

Tom explained his work in Iraq with the same philosophy of aiding others. "There are many people who are willing to die for war. There must be more people who are willing to die for peace."

How much did Americans send to Pakistan or Iraq in their hour of need? Was it proportional to our wealth? After September 11, 2001, people in Iran held public vigils for our victims. Did we cry in the streets at the pictures of the suffering from the white phosphorous sprayed on innocent families in Fallujah? Or the crushed victims in Pakistan? How did we become so numb?

Tom reflected on these choices between apathy, fear, and anger in his journal. *"It seems easier somehow to confront anger within my heart than it is to confront fear. But if Jesus and Gandhi are right then I am not to give in to either. I am to stand firm*

74

against the kidnapper as I am to stand firm against the soldier. Does that mean I walk into a raging battle to confront the soldiers? Does that mean I walk the streets of Baghdad with a sign saying "American for the Taking"? No to both counts. But if Jesus and Gandhi are right, then I am asked to risk my life and if I lose it to be as forgiving as they were when murdered . . . . I struggle to stand firm but I'm willing to keep working at it."

Tom was my student in the "Strategic Nonviolence" course here at EMU in 2004. He was my third student to die because of his work for peace. When I look out at my classrooms of students now, their faces and stories are all the more precious to me.

The blood-soaked sands in Iraq seem far away from shopping centers in North America. Real security for Iraqis and Americans will depend on the long term work that Tom and many others will do in Iraq and other places around the world to offer hope. Like the poor woman reaching into her purse, we must keep asking, like Tom did, "what do I have to give and can I be brave enough to give it?"

Lisa Schirch is an associate professor of peacebuilding at Eastern Mennonite University. A former Fulbright Fellow, Schirch has worked in over a dozen countries as a researcher, trainer, and facilitator in the fields of conflict transformation and peacebuilding for 15 years. Dr. Schirch is the director of the 3-D Security Campaign for the Center for Justice & Peacebuilding.

Recommended books:

Lisa Schirch. *The Little Book of Strategic Peacebuilding*. PA: Good Books, 2005.

James Gilligan. *Preventing Violence*. New York: Thames and Hudson. 2001.

20. The Road to Syria

Tom – Wednesday, October 26, 2005

From Oct. 4th until Oct. 17th CPTers accompanied and then stayed with a group of nineteen Palestinians living in Baghdad who decided to try to gain refuge in Syria: refuge from the night raids, arbitrary arrests and torture-induced confessions their community has been subject to by Iraqi security forces for eight months. They are still camped out at the Syrian border awaiting news from the Syrian government as to whether or not they can enter Syria since their status since 1948 as "guests" in Iraq does not allow them to enter neighboring countries.

Tuesday, October 4th - It is midday and the temperature in this desert region of eastern Iraq is around one hundred degrees Fahrenheit. Nineteen Palestinians from Iraq, three CPTers, their translator and one member of the Muslim Peacemaker Teams have just spent the night sleeping on the sidewalk at the Al Walid border crossing between Syria and Iraq. People have enough water, but the intense heat is still taking its toll on the men, women and children. There are dozens of tractor-trailers waiting to cross the border. One of the drivers sees the group and pulls his rig close to the sidewalk, creating a protective shadow for shade.

Thursday, October 6th - The UN has arranged for the community to have two meals per day at the border-crossing cafeteria. The Syrian cafeteria manager is talking to community members about how things are going. One person mentions that there is very little to do as they await word from the Syrian government regarding their status. Soon afterwards a soccer ball appears and is given to the community. Both children and adults find it a welcome source of recreation.

Tuesday, October 11th - The Syrian government still refuses to allow any of the Palestinians to enter Syria as refugees. Two members of the community pay a social call to one of the Syrian officials in charge of the border crossing. At the conclusion of their visit they invite the officer to come meet everyone at the camp. He arrives several hours later as members of the community are gathered under the star-filled sky next to a roaring campfire. Community members offer him tea and the conversation goes on late into the night.

Jennifer Elam

A Godly Play Story About Tom Fox

Materials:

Mat

Peace symbol

4 figures holding hands in a circle

paper or felt shaped like Iraq

the letters I R A Q

children's figures

paper shadows

double heart

tent

figure sitting and reading a book

tea candles

matches

The story:

Today I want to tell you about a Quaker man named Tom Fox who believed in walking cheerfully over the earth answering to that of God in everyone.

Put out the mat

77

Tom was a dad. He had 2 children, a girl and a boy. Tom loved his children and loved being a dad. He loved to cook and he loved making music.

And he loved peace. Tom Fox was a peacemaker.

Put out the peace symbol.

One day Tom heard God ask him to go to a place where there was war, a place that really needed peacemakers.

(Optional for those who have studied the Godly Play stories:

This is a place we have been before. This part of the world is now called the Middle East and is where Jesus came from. Abram lived here. Moses lived here. This is where the Family of God came from. An area near the desert that Abram and Moses came from became the villages and cities of what is now called Iraq. After the Family of God, there came many other families. They had children who had children who had children until your grandparents were born and they had your parents and your parents had you. And other families had children who had children until the grandparents were born; they had the parents of the children now in this land called Iraq. And now there is a war in Iraq. This is where God's people began and we are going back there. We all came from there and Tom Fox felt called to go back. Abram was called to the desert. Moses was called to the desert. And Tom Fox was called to the desert).

Tom joined with other peacemakers who felt God wanted them to go to a place where there was war. They formed a team and were called a Christian Peacemaker Team.

Put the 4 guys together holding hands on the right side of the mat.

Tom's team called themselves a Christian team because, like Jesus, they believed that people need to love and forgive one another. People are different from one another and may not understand one another. They may have conflicts but they need to work out differences without being violent and hurting one another. Christian Peacemaker Teams believe that our world would be a lot better place if we all put our energy into making peace instead of making war.

While putting out the piece shaped like Iraq and the letters
I R A Q

The land that God wanted Tom to go to was called Iraq. Tom listened to God and went there. When he got to Iraq, Tom saw many people hurting and killing one another. Many children were being hurt and they were sad. *Put out the sad children* Tom was especially concerned about the children because they did not have the food or medicine they needed.

Put out double heart.

When Tom was in Iraq, he was faithful to what God asked him to do. His friends said he was gentle, patient, compassionate, forgiving and courageous. His heart met the hearts of the Iraqi people.

While putting up the tent, placing Tom sitting in front with a book.

Sometimes he lived in a tent and sat by his tent and read books to people that would help them to be more loving and forgiving. Sometimes he cooked them delicious food. Sometimes he just listened to their stories and they felt loved by him. His voice made the people less afraid. He might say, "I am glad I am here to help." Or he might say, "You keep taking care of yourself now." And his friends felt less afraid.

When people are hurting and killing one another, many people feel mad and afraid. Tom prayed for all of the people, those doing the hurting and those being hurt, and that helped him not to be mad at people. Being afraid was even harder to overcome than feeling mad. Almost everyday he prayed, did yoga and welcomed the sun as it came up in the morning. He said thank you to God for his life and all that he was given. And that made Tom feel less afraid.

One day when Tom was sitting in meeting for worship, an image came to him about Iraq. Tom saw that Iraq was "a land of shadows and darkness.

Put black pieces for shadows across the land.

But within that land candles were burning; not many candles but enough to shed some light on the landscape.

Put candles up slowly.

Some candles disappeared –

Take away candles.

– and it was my sense that their light was taken away for protection. Other candles burned until nothing was left and a small number of candles seemed to have their light snuffed out by the shadows and darkness.

What was most striking was that as the candles which burned until the end and the candles whose light was snuffed out ceased to burn, more candles came into being, seemingly to build on their light."

Put up many more candles.

Tom said, "there are many people willing to die for war. There must be more people who are willing to die for peace."

He knew he was in a dangerous land and that he could be hurt or killed because many people around him were being hurt and killed. When he talked with his friends about the possibility of his being hurt or killed, he said, "If I am ever called upon to make the ultimate sacrifice in love of enemy, I trust that God will give me the grace to do so." Soon after that he was kidnapped and then killed.

(Pause.) Take Tom out of the picture.

His friends say that they are sure that Tom forgave those who did it.

Place hands over each group as you say the following words:

People everywhere were sad when Tom died; his children were very sad, his friends were sad, the people in Iraq were sad, the children were sad, and people on both sides of the fighting were sad. Many people were sad who did not know Tom but knew of his work. They knew that Tom was a Quaker and lived a good life. Tom wanted to live like Jesus, and he did in many ways. And people in many places in the world said, "If Tom can be faithful to his calling to be a peacemaker, I can too. I can live more simply."

Hold a cross in your hand (if the group is uncomfortable with the cross symbol, a candle/light could be used)

Tom believed deeply that there is that of God in EVERY person. Some people call that of God in every person (the Light or) Christ-energy. Some people believe that Christ-energy keeps on living even if the person dies. That of God was in Tom and Tom's (light) Christ-energy is here, inspiring us. Tom followed Jesus as his example.

Place the cross (or candle), the heart and the peace symbol on the front of the mat.

Another man named George Fox started Quakerism. He told us to "be patterns, be examples in every country, place, or nation that you visit then you'll walk cheerfully across the earth and help bring to light that of God in everybody. You will be seen as a blessing in their eyes and you will receive a blessing from that of God within them." Tom felt blessed as he worked happily with the people in Iraq. Tom Fox followed his teacher George Fox and he was a peacemaker.

Tom Fox lived as he believed was right. And he died. BUT THAT IS NOT THE END OF THE STORY! Tom saw that when one candle goes out, many more get lit. Others will become peacemakers and follow Tom as an example, just as Tom and George Fox followed Jesus. Set up more candles.

Sit quietly for a moment.

In silence, light the candles and leave them lit while doing the wondering questions.

Wonderings

- I wonder what part of the story you liked best?
- I wonder how you might be a peacemaker in your life today?
- I wonder if you have ever been a peacemaker?
- I wonder what you might do as a peacemaker when you are a grown-up?
- I wonder if it was hard for Tom Fox to forgive people that hurt him?
- I wonder what the candles in the story represent?
- I wonder what is the most important part of the story for you?
- I wonder where you are in the story. I wonder what part of the story is about you?

■ I wonder where is God in the story?

I am going to put the story of Tom Fox away. These lights are burning for peace. Even when I blow them out, in our hearts, they are still burning for peace.

Jennifer Elam is a member of Berea Friends Meeting in Kentucky but has lived in Pennsylvania for the past ten years and now attends Goshen Meeting near Philadelphia. She works as a school psychologist in early intervention with preschoolers. She has felt called to work within Quakerism doing writing and painting, leading retreats in arts and spirituality. A decade ago she felt led to listen to people's stories of their experiences of God and write about those stories. She wrote a Pendle Hill pamphlet called "Dancing with God," then followed with a book, *Dancing with God through the Storm: Mysticism and Mental Illness.* Since then she wrote: "Are You There God or Am I Going Crazy?", "Humanity Emerging," and "My Angel Came."

Godly Play was developed by Jerome W. Berryman, an episcopal clergyman. His *Complete Guide to Godly Play* (in several volumes), is published by Living the Good Life in Denver, Colorado.

21. Seeking a Unified Vision

Tom – Monday, February 14, 2005

. . . The force of war has three central aspects. First it requires a tremendous deal of energy. Both external, physical energy and the internal drive to carry out the external aspects. Second it requires tremendous organization and teamwork. To take on the implementation of a war plan requires a great number of human beings working together. Third it requires a unified vision of purpose. Goals must be established and everyone plays a part in their successful outcome.

Unified vision, teamwork and energy are all very good things to make use of to bring about the creation of the Peaceable Realm. But in the case of warfare all of these aspects come from a reverse image–and that reverse image comes from the negative, parasitic energy of Satan. Satan acts as a mimic of God but a mimic guiding us in the opposite way. It functions just as a mirror reverses everything it displays. Instead of compassion there is vengeance; instead of justice tempered with mercy there is redemptive violence. Creativity is harnessed to discover new and more effective ways to kill each other instead of working to discover new and more effective ways of communicating with each other.

This force of war is evident no matter which side of a conflict a country finds itself. The country that attacks or the country that defends uses the same force. As is chess the rules of the game are the same for white, the aggressor, and black, the defender.

Is it possible that this force is in reality a negative, mirror image of the force of peace? And is it also possible that the major difference is that the false, mirror image leads a person, or country

84

or ethnic group to walk away from God and towards the contagion of Satan. Can we defeat the power of Satan by working to create a true image that draws that person, nation or ethnic group into a relationship of walking towards God?

. . . The negative mirror image of war can be reversed and begin to be seen as the true image of peace but it will take many, many people being willing "to turn, turn, turn till by turning, turning we come round right" (from the Shaker tune "Simple Gifts"). Only then would our world-view direct all our energy towards God and none towards Satan.

A Letter Received at Quaker House, Fayetteville-Ft. Bragg North Carolina, two days before a peace rally on the third anniversary of the US invasion of Iraq..

March 16, 2006

Dear Mr. Fager:

"Blessed are the peacemakers, for they will be called sons of God." Mt 5:9

I am writing to say that I am so very sorry to know that your friend was killed in Iraq. I, too, have lost friends in Iraq and can sympathize with the sorrow and loss you are surely feeling at this time. I did not know Tom Fox personally, and only know what I've read about him, but by all accounts he was a brave man committed to a cause he was prepared to die for as were my friends. He is said to have been a man of faith, driven by a desire to imitate the heart of Christ by improving the condition of men everywhere as were my friends. I am sickened to learn that Rush Limbaugh made comments delighting in your friend's death.* Thankfully, few people take Rush Limbaugh seriously. (I'm ashamed to admit that I delighted in his hearing loss, however I saw that as an extremely funny joke played by God.)

God, through his son Jesus Christ, desired peace on Earth for all people – the new Testament of the Bible makes this quite clear. I am not Quaker myself, but one of my oldest, dearest, friends was raised Quaker and I attended many Friends meetings with her. I admire the Quaker beliefs and the spirit of most Quakers I've met. I say all this to implore you to be a true peacemaker.

It is my sincere belief that you are not pursuing peace here, in Fayetteville, particularly with regard to Saturday's protest and rally. That is an event designed to instigate and orchestrated to offend the majority of the people who live here. If you are not a peacemaker in your own land   how can you call for peace elsewhere?

I live in the Haymount [neighborhood] and last year's march passed close by my house. I saw marchers carrying Styrofoam coffins – symbolic of the people who have died in Iraq. I asked one of the girls who carried the coffins why she was carrying it. She told me, "So people will remember that war kills." No one in this community.needs to be reminded of that. Elsewhere in the U.S., perhaps, but not here. I buried eight dear friends last year and have buried two more already this year. Most people in Fayetteville have some connection to someone who has been killed in this war. We do not need to be reminded.

Honestly, I think it is a smug arrogance on the part of the protesters that draws them to our town to tell us what we should think to tell us what is happening in Iraq as if our own husbands' and neighbors' firsthand accounts are not to be trusted. As you can probably tell, I get very angry when I think about the protesters coming here. Certainly you all have a right to express your opinions – but I have to question your motives when you choose to do so here. Angering people for the sake of angering them is not making the peace.

Sincerely,

A Special Forces Wife

* *Shortly after Tom and his colleagues were kidnaped, radio host Rush Limbaugh commented: "Part of me likes this," because, "I like any time a bunch of leftist feel-good hand-wringers are shown reality."*

Some Comments from a Tennessee weblog,
December 2005 and January 2006:
Re: Tom Fox, Humanitarian Worker and Peace Activist, Held
     Hostage in Iraq for Seventh Day by **xxxxx**

06 Dec 2005 *"We are here to stop people, including ourselves, from dehumanizing any of God's children, no matter how much they dehumanize their own souls."*

Unfortunatly, these folks holding you don't feel this way. They don't care how well meaning you're intentions are or anything else.

To them, you are nothing but an infidel. If you are not one of them, then you are nothing less than a dog. That's what these people you want to help have been brainwashed to believe since birth. No amount of wishful thinking of world peace or everyone getting along and singing Kum-by-ya is going to change this.

They are motivated by one thing: the killing or conversion of anyone who is not just like them. They care about nothing else but death.

I can't believe these people were actually stupid enough to travel to a hot war zone to "spread the love." They might as well as stood in downtown Baghdad with a sign that says "PLEASE BEHEAD ME – I AM A NAIVE FOOL"

Because that is exactly what is going to happen. These monsters don't give a damn about their silly yet noble intentions.

Unless our armed forces get some really good intelligence on their whereabouts and quickly, any day now, we're going be hearing a breaking news story on CNN about a terrible videotape just aired on Al Jazeera...

. . . and then all you dope smoking, peace and love types will blame it all on Bush...

87

. . . as usual.

What a fucking waste. They should have stayed home.

Re: Tom Fox, Peace Activist and Former Chattanoogan, Remains Hostage in Iraq, by **yyyyy**

10 Dec 2005 I gasped when I heard the voice on the other end of the phone say that one of my former fellow Chattanooga High School band members was being held hostage in Iraq. When the news reporter asked me what I knew about Tom Fox, I replied that he was a bit odd (that doesn't seem to have changed), quiet and a nice person. I certainly didn't say he deserved what he may or may not be getting. Liberal or conservative, most of you people and especially Limbaugh, need to get a life. Even now, I don't agree with all of Tom's writing and I'm not so sure I even can label his "theology" as "Christian". That does not, however, give me or you all the gavel to go around banging (while this man sits in a part of the world that will know no peace until Jesus Himself puts His foot on the Mount of Olives)and proclaiming judgement on him when you yourselves are probably doing precious little to improve the quality of society in which we live.

Congratulations M------. You seem to have the proper response to this whole mess. Several of you need to get your mouths washed out with soap and your hands stuck down into a bucket of battery acid. It may improve your concept of the King's English.

Whatever happens to Tom(whether he should or should not have been there) God have mercy on his soul.

Re: Tom Fox, Peace Activist and Former Chattanoogan, Remains Hostage in Iraq, by Ccccc

28 Jan 2006 As a member of a Pacifist church, I am very supportive of CPT (Christian Peacamaker Teams). Very few people have this level of courage or commitment, to risk their lives to help others. It saddens me to hear anyone degrade or ridicule the captive CPTer's. They are my heroes.

29117722R00067

Made in the USA
Middletown, DE
09 February 2016